Flying Ultralights

Instructional Briefings

DISCARD

Doug Chipman

Foreword by Amy Laboda

Aviation Supplies & Academics, Inc.
Newcastle, Washington

U.S. Edition 1995
Published by Aviation Supplies & Academics, Inc.

©1995 Center for Aviation Theory

Flying Ultralights
Doug Chipman

ASA-ULF
ISBN 1-56027-218-X

Aviation Supplies & Academics, Inc.
7005 132nd Place SE
Newcastle, Washington 98059-3153

Printed in the United States of America

9 8 7 6 5 4 3

Acknowledgments

This manual has been prepared to support the rapidly developing ultralight aviation industry. It has been developed from flight instructor's manuals I have used for other aircraft, and after personal instructional experience on ultralight aircraft. The aim was to transfer the body of professional knowledge about flying instruction, already in the public domain, in a meaningful way to ultralight pilots and instructors.

While I take full responsibility for the final product, I am very grateful to Harry Walton and Chris Mills, ultralight instructors, for their encouragement and advice during its preparation. Rod Birrell and Stan Jarman also offered excellent advice.

I am grateful to my wife Jo for her persistence with the word processor and to Lou Emmett for her photographic support.

Finally, Trevor Thom's professionalism, patience and editorial expertise assisted me greatly in refining this manual. Without the help of all of these people I'm sure that this publication could not have been possible.

Doug Chipman

Contents

About the Author

Doug Chipman began his career as a military student pilot and has flown the Macchi jet trainer, Caribou STOL transport aircraft and C-130H Hercules. As a professional flying instructor, he acquired considerable instructional experience on Winjeel, CT-4 and other light aircraft. He has accumulated over 5,000 hours as a pilot and flies now as a part-time instructor on ultralight aircraft as a hobby— one that he finds both challenging and interesting.

Editor

Amy Laboda is a freelance writer, editor, active flight instructor, and member of the American Flyers Judith Resnik Scholarship committee. A former editor at Flying magazine, she has rotorcraft category, and ratings in gyroplane, glider, and multiengine ATP. She holds a B.A. in Liberal Arts from Sarah Lawrence College.

Foreword

You won't get much closer to what the birds feel than in an ultralight aircraft. There is nothing like firing up the engine of your gossamer-winged machine on a clear, cool, calm morning and rolling out onto a dew-covered grass field for takeoff. Once aloft your visibility may be unrestricted, and you can feel the air rushing around your body and over your flying helmet. The engine hums quietly behind you as the world below opens to your view. It is unquestionably the definition of pure, clean fun.

For most of us, ultralights provide an affordable, exciting and safe introduction to the broad field of aviation. The United States ultralight movement is strong, expanding and currently produces many well-constructed new aircraft, most of which do not require a pilot's certificate of the person who flies them. The current Federal Aviation Administration regulations state that any craft that carries only one person, five gallons of fuel, has an empty weight less than 254 pounds, a maximum calibrated airspeed of 55 knots at full power in level flight, and has a power-off stall speed of less than 24 knots calibrated airspeed, is considered an ultralight if it is used purely for sports and recreational purposes.

Although there are no federal regulations regarding pilot or instructor certification in ultralight aircraft, you must be a skilled aviator to operate these machines. The United States Ultralight Association (USUA), located in Frederick, Maryland, has more than 100 ultralight clubs and/or airfields on its roster. In 1992 the USUA took the initiative and created an ultralight pilot and instructor certification program of its own, which has been voluntarily submitted to by more than 400 certified ultralight flight instructors, who are now registered in the USUA national registry.

Doug Chipman's manual of instructional briefings is designed to aid both the ultralight instructor and the enthusiast just learning to fly. Instructors will be delighted by the tightly organized, detailed exercises, explanations and illustrations for how to fly an ultralight aircraft.

Flying an ultralight is different than flying a heavier, faster certified aircraft, therefore teaching someone to fly an ultralight is different, too. This manual contains sections on emergency procedures, stalls, spins, navigation and formation flying that are tailored to the express needs of the ultralight recreational flier. Instructors can find the information they want to teach without having to edit out extraneous information meant for students working toward an FAA pilot certificate and without having to contradict procedures listed in the text. This means there is little confusion among the instructor, student and study manual as to how to proceed with flight training.

Students who use this manual will find that is shortens the time it takes them to learn to fly by giving them a comprehensive reference that they can share with their instructor and by helping them prepare for each flight lesson.

There are few texts directed solely at the recreational ultralight aviator. This book is sure to become the ultralight instructor pilot's hip-pocket guide.

Amy Laboda

Introduction

While this handbook presents ultralight pilots with a complete guide to ultralight flying training, it is not a substitute for personal experience and in no way removes from the individual the right to use his or her own initiative. Neither does it usurp any recommendations made by the United States Ultralight Association (USUA), aircraft manufacturers' manuals nor aircraft owners' operating procedures.

This handbook provides useful advice to instructors in the form of *A Note to the Ultralight Instructor* and a set of training sequences referred to as *Exercises.* Because the handbook will be of greatest benefit to those who understand how to use it correctly, some explanation of the layout is provided in the following paragraphs.

Regarding the Note to the Ultralight Instructor (page ix)

The principles of flight instruction are broadly similar to those of tuition in other fields, and apply equally at all stages of training. However, since the object is not only to teach the student to fly the aircraft, but also to understand its capabilities, the flight instructor must combine the roles of tutor, demonstrator and lecturer, depending on whether he or she is briefing before or after flight, demonstrating in the air or lecturing theory to a group. It is a task which demands good technique, and the advice contained in the *Note to the Ultralight Instructor* is designed to assist in the development of that technique.

The Note comprises general comments on instruction, an explanation of the ideal instructional sequence, a discussion about the qualities of flying instructors, a discussion about the nature of students and a suggested syllabus.

The Exercises

This Handbook comprises of a series of Exercises, each of which encompasses, as appropriate, a teaching *Objective* for the instructor, *Considerations* applicable to teaching the exercise, pertinent points of *Airmanship,* an *Air Exercise* sequence of maneuvers or activities, and finally, a section entitled *Post-Flight Discussion.*

Objective

The *Objective,* as stated at the commencement of each exercise, gives an overall picture of just what the instructor is ultimately endeavoring to teach the student.

Considerations

The section entitled *Considerations,* apart from containing advice on teaching the exercise, provides a summary of the theory with which students should be familiar before they are instructed in the exercise. It also contains a list of significant preflight briefing points which should be discussed. This manual does not attempt to explain theoretical knowledge which should be familiar to ultralight students before they attempt the practical exercises. *Flight Training* published by *Aviation Supplies & Academics, Inc.* contains this knowledge and is, I feel, a suitable reference for use by student ultralight pilots in conjunction with this manual. This book can be obtained from an aviation bookshop by quoting the ASA stock code number which is ASA-PM-1.

Airmanship

The section entitled *Airmanship* contains points which are relevant to the exercise concerned. Airmanship is the ability to choose the most effective and safest course of action for a particular set of circumstances. It is important that the student's sense of airmanship, apart from his or her individual skill, should be developed so that he or she is able to recognize the approach of a potentially dangerous situation in good time. The student should be made aware of the fact that common sense and airmanship are synonymous, and that their use implies careful planning and continuous anticipation.

Air Exercise

The section entitled *Air Exercise* lists the **skills** which are to be achieved, the **techniques** required to achieve these skills, and any **observations** which the student should be invited to note at a suitable moment during the flight.

Post-Flight Discussion

The Post-Flight Discussion is used to review the exercise and amplify or explain any special point(s) of interest or difficulty that has arisen. The discussion is invaluable for consolidating what the student has just learned. The section contains a list of the more common faults made by students, and advice on how to correct them.

A Note to the Ultralight Instructor

General Notes on Instruction

Learning to fly consists of accumulating a store of knowledge and skill. Exercises are explained, demonstrated and practiced until the student is able to react quickly and instinctively to ordinary problems without having to resort to laborious elementary reasoning; the solutions are provided from the store of ready answers which has been accumulated through experience. This principle also applies to most other forms of practical training, but since flying demands quick thinking from the outset, the student must be especially free to concentrate on his or her task.

The attitude of the instructor toward his or her student can have a significant effect on the student's rate of progress. The instructor should spare no effort to stimulate interest and enthusiasm by teaching in a way that holds the interest. The rate of progress varies between students, but the successful accomplishment of each new exercise serves as a useful spur to further effort.

The student must be made to feel that he or she is subject to benevolent discipline in congenial surroundings. The wise instructor will readily appreciate that attention to the comfort and welfare of the student will be amply repaid in trust and respect and that the greater receptivity to instruction thus engendered makes the task much easier. If any feeling of antipathy or incompatibility is sensed in the instructor/student relationship, the student should be put in the hands of another instructor; if this is not done the student's progress may be affected to the extent of complete failure to progress.

Flying instruction should be confined to the simple facts, and full use made of available aids to instruction, for example blackboard, models, diagrams, and so on. The student learns through the use of all of his or her senses and the instructor should draw attention to all the sensations involved in an exercise; for example, the student can see the changing attitude, hear the changing engine note and air flow noise, and feel the response of the aircraft to control movements.

In a briefing do not bore the student by trying to write down everything you say, but highlight the important points so that he or she can form a mental picture of the subject. Quote examples and analogies whenever possible, especially if the student finds discussion and explanations difficult to follow.

The Instructional Sequence

Theory

Theoretical instruction on Basic Aircraft Knowledge and Rules of the Air must be provided to the student in parallel with his or her flight lessons. Each particular theory lesson should be given before its associated air exercise is briefed and flown. Theory lessons may be conducted by the students as self-paced tutorials from recognized theory manuals.

Preparation

Prepare every lesson thoroughly so that you know exactly what you have to teach and how you are going to teach it. Study the objective of the exercise and keep it constantly in mind.

The flight should be planned to give the student the maximum benefit without making excessive demands on his or her concentration and limited experience. Each lesson should follow as a logical development of the preceding lessons. The instructor should ensure that the conditions under which each new exercise is introduced are such that the student is not distracted by irrelevant matters or subjected to extra difficulty. For example, the first flights should be planned so that the student has a reasonably well defined physical horizon, making any attempt to fly straight-and-level that much easier.

The Pre-Flight Briefing

The pre-flight briefing, which is given before each flight, should provide the link between the theory already learned and the air exercise. It should also cover such details as the effect of weather on the flight, any unusual obstacles or restrictions in the circuit traffic pattern area and on the airfield, and similar information. An overview of the main points of the lesson about to be taught must be included: these points can be based on the relevant observations in the air exercise.

In Flight

The student's active participation in the lesson is all important. He or she should be allowed to take control of the aircraft as soon as possible when learning a new exercise because **a student learns mostly by practice**. You should normally take over only to give demonstrations, when the student needs a rest or when he or she obviously cannot cope with a situation. To this end, the essentials should be taught first and the refinements dealt with after the student has completed the exercise.

The habit of critical self-analysis of the student's flying should be encouraged. This involves the student being able to identify accurately what the aircraft did, explain why, and then induce how to make any corrections that are necessary. To develop this process you should, whenever advantageous, ask questions which necessitate the use of such critical reasoning; more is achieved in this way than a series of bald, critical statements.

Post-Flight Briefing

Never fail, however briefly, to discuss the flight with the student immediately after leaving the aircraft. Post-flight discussion gives an opportunity to advise on any difficulties while they are still fresh in the student's mind; it is also an important indication of the instructor's interest, without which the student is likely to feel that his or her progress is of little consequence.

Qualities of Flight Instructors

The qualities which make a good flight instructor are acquired rather than innate, and many pilots who originally doubted that they had the necessary flair for teaching have, in fact, become extremely capable instructors. The technique is developed largely through contact with students and their problems, but this Manual is written primarily for the new instructor who lacks the benefit of experience. The most important attributes of an instructor are discussed in the following paragraphs. They should be read, not as a matter of passing interest, but as a basis for improvement and periodical self-analysis.

Skill

The instructor must be able to fly the aircraft at all times with a high degree of accuracy. Besides having to give demonstrations in a skillful and convincing manner, the instructor must remember that the student learns by example and will quickly imitate bad habits as well as good ones.

Knowledge

To explain a subject clearly it is necessary to know more about it than must be taught; instructors should therefore keep themselves well-informed on all subjects related to pure flying training.

Discipline

The student looks to the instructor on the ground, as well as in the air, for an example of what a good pilot should be; a student expects a high standard of professional conduct, and any lapse is likely to make a permanent impression. The relationship between the two should nevertheless be an easy one in which problems of any kind can be freely aired. There should be an atmosphere of friendly authority that encourages frank discussion.

Expression

Instructors must be able to speak distinctly and express themselves clearly. Explanations should be made at a leisurely pace which is easy to follow, and the voice should be kept at a pitch that makes every word audible without strain.

Patience

Students learn at their own pace and even when doing their best forget a great deal of what has been taught. Many points are driven home only after constant repetition, and failure to grasp them readily should never be made the occasion for displays of impatience by the instructor; such outbursts usually result only in anxiety or bewilderment. Instructors should rather assume that they are using the wrong method, and approach the problem from a different angle.

Restraint

There are always times when a student seems especially slow to learn and often a whole training session may appear to have been wasted. Such experiences can prove extremely exasperating, but it must be remembered that no purpose will be served by giving way to anger. If reproach is necessary it is most effectively delivered in a restrained and reasoned manner.

Understanding

The instructor must understand the problems of the student and treat them in a sympathetic and helpful manner. It is possible for the student's enthusiasm to be completely undermined by brooding on some difficulty which might easily be solved after a little sound advice. The instructor must often be something of a psychologist, although all that is required in most cases is an active interest in the student.

Adaptability

Since all students differ in their method and rate of learning, the instructor must be able to distinguish between students and adapt his or her approach to the individual. It is also important to fit the personal treatment of each student to the temperament of that particular student; even a mild rebuke can sound extremely harsh to a sensitive character, whereas criticism might need to be extremely forthright to impress a headstrong student.

Personality

There is a tendency among some inexperienced instructors to use a rather formal approach to instruction—particularly in the air. This makes their demonstrations monotonous and uninteresting. It might well be that their instructional information is very good but the impersonal atmosphere can turn what should be enjoyable into a dull experience for the student.

Everyone has their own distinct personality, and the instructor should use the best possible to capture the interest of the student. Brief digression and touches of humor do much to relieve the strain during some of the more demanding exercises and encourage the student to renewed efforts. It is important that instructors should infect the student with their own enthusiasm for flying.

Just as there are rules which should be followed by instructors, there are errors which must be avoided. It is possible to avoid most of them by using ordinary discretion and common sense, but a few of the more common errors, often made with the best of intentions, are worth mentioning.

Verbosity

Never talk too much in the air. Put over the important points and give the student a chance to absorb them. Avoid lengthy explanations. Note the points which require further elucidation and discuss them on the ground.

Excessive Criticism

Do not criticize every single mistake your student makes. Concentrate initially on any major errors and work your way down to the minor ones as the student improves. Never confine criticism to mere factual indications but explain or analyze the reasons for mistakes whenever possible.

Subterfuge

Never try to gloss over or disguise your own mistakes; students are not likely to be taken in and will respect you far more if you admit an error and give them a chance to learn from it by pointing out how it should have been avoided.

Ostentation

It is a good thing to whet the student's appetite for flying by showing him what the aircraft can do in capable hands, but such demonstrations must be kept within reason. Even the most enthusiastic student can lose confidence in an instructor after an intimidating or foolhardy exhibition of flying.

The Nature of Students

All students come to their instructor after volunteering to learn to fly and this initiative is of great advantage to the instructor. If, consequently, the student shows an unduly slow rate of progress, then it may be a symptom of some more deep-rooted difficulty, such as a basic fear of flying.

Students differ so widely in nature and ability that it is difficult even to attempt to categorize them. Some of the more common traits, however, are outlined below.

Overconfidence

A conceited student often displays a degree of confidence which is not borne out by his or her ability. The instructor should insist relentlessly on a high standard of accuracy and airmanship, criticizing all imperfection in a firm but fair manner so that the student is constantly aware of shortcomings.

A more difficult case occasionally arises in which a feeling of inferiority or insecurity is cloaked in an attitude of aggressiveness; the subject may betray himself by nervous gestures or mannerisms when off guard. This complex requires careful handling, since repressing the apparent overconfidence may only aggravate the cause.

Under-Confidence

Nervous, diffident students need encouragement. They tend to be extremely self-critical and become discouraged if not assured that progress is normal. Students should be praised freely when doing well, and mistakes should be explained carefully without undue reflection on their ability. Care must be taken in the air to avoid any signs of apprehension while the student is in control of the aircraft.

Forgetfulness

Most students forget a great deal of what they are taught and facts must be ingrained by constant revision. Leaving ordinary carelessness or neglect aside, instances of genuinely poor memory are frequently encountered. Forgetful students should be made to take a very active part during dual instruction and should be called upon to recount on the ground what they have learned in the air. Faulty checks should be corrected and the student made to repeat the correct procedure in its entirety.

Inconsistency

The process of learning is an irregular one, and many instructors are discouraged when they find their students becoming stale from time to time. This is because the mind can become saturated with new ideas and the student's receptivity often deteriorates until the fresh information has been consolidated in his or her memory.

Flying training takes place in an entirely new medium and it is not uncommon for some students to make a slow start only to progress rapidly at a later stage when they feel more at home. It is therefore unwise to worry unduly if a student appears to stand still for a while; when this occurs it is best to revise the earlier lessons until the student has recovered his or her place. A lengthy lapse, however, is usually due to some more profound difficulty and requires closer investigation.

Apathy

If a student becomes unusually slow, inattentive, or erratic, it can be due to a number of troubles. It may, of course, be mere backsliding but it would be wrong to assume this without having investigated the case. It is always possible that he or she may be distracted by some personal problem—the instructor should try to discover the difficulty as tactfully as possible.

The most common reasons for loss of enthusiasm are private worries, distaste for flying, or personal antipathy between student and instructor.

Private Worries

Domestic or financial problems can be very distracting and the student is usually reluctant to discuss them, particularly if they are of an emotional nature.

Distaste for Flying

Students who have been quite keen sometimes lose the zest for flying because of adverse comments about the aircraft they are flying, or another type which they are likely to fly. On the other hand, they may have been shaken by an incident involving themselves or another student.

Students will seldom admit loss of confidence, but often portray it by expressing a dislike for the aircraft, some aspect of flying or by a general loss of interest. Such students need careful treatment and must be reassured by all possible means. Rumors can usually be exposed as *perversions of the truth* and it can be explained that serious accidents are rare and become even less likely as skill and experience increase.

The condition is usually a passing phase but it sometimes happens, fortunately rarely, that the student has suddenly realized that he or she has no stomach for flying; in this case there is no alternative but to discontinue the training.

Personal Antipathy

A clash of personalities can destroy the sympathetic atmosphere which is essential between student and instructor. Therefore, if the student fails to progress, particularly in the early stages, and there is reason to believe that this may be the cause, a change of instructor should be made without delay.

Suggested Syllabus of Training

The suggested syllabus of training (which follows) contains a series of lessons with suggested exercise content and flight time (dual and solo). The syllabus represents the maximum progress that a student could be expected to make. **It cannot be emphasized too strongly** that each student's ability to learn will vary and that times shown are simply illustrative. *Each lesson must in fact be carried out until the required standard is achieved, regardless of the flying time involved.*

In the initial demonstration of an Exercise it may be unwise to attempt to cover all the observations. The intensity of the instruction given should be tailored to the ability of the student—the aim being eventually to cover all the points in a reasonable time. Note that the order in which the observations are given is not a reflection of their importance—all are equally important—but their order is logical if all the comments are made in a single demonstration.

In addition, the order in which the exercises are demonstrated and carried out may be varied to suit existing weather and other conditions.

Suggested Syllabus of Training

Lesson Number	Suggested Content	Suggested Time (hrs)	
		Dual	Solo
1	**Exercises 1, 2, 3 & 4** The air experience aspects of this lesson will be continued until the student is sufficiently relaxed to be receptive to further instruction. Then introduce 'The Controls' exercise. The extent to which the demonstrations are covered will depend on the aptitude of the student and the time available.	.4	
2	**Exercises 2, 4, 5, 6 & 9** Repetition and completion of 'The Controls'. Introduction to straight-and-level, turning and taxiing.	.4	
3	**Exercises 5, 6, 7, 8 & 9** Demonstration of new sequences for climbing, descending, gliding turns and climbing turns. Practice taxiing, straight-and-level flight and level turns.	.5	
4	**Exercises 6, 7, 8, 9 & 10** Demonstration of stalling. Practice level, climbing and descending turns.	.5	
5	**Exercises 10, 12 & 13** Practice stalling. Demonstrate and practice circuits.	.5	
6	**Exercises 10, 12 & 13** Review of stalling. Demonstration of glide circuit traffic patterns. Practice normal and patterns.	.7	

Lesson Number	Suggested Content	Suggested Time (hrs)	
		Dual	Solo
7	**Exercises 12 & 13** Demonstrate simulated engine failures after takeoff. Practice normal and glide circuits.	.7	
8–11	Practice circuits until the student is ready for his first solo.	2.2	.2
12	Dual check the solo in the circuit.	.2	.5
13	Dual check the solo in the circuit.	.2	.5
14	Solo circuits.		.7
15	**Exercises 8, 10, 15 & 17** Demonstrate practice forced landings. Introduce steep turns and sideslipping. Practice sideslipping. Review stalling.	.7	
16	Practice stalls, steep turns, sideslipping and circuits.		.7
17	Practice stalls, steep turns, sideslipping and circuits.		.7
18	Practice forced landings and steep turns. Introduce maximum rate and angle climbing.	.5	
19	Practice forced landings and steep turns. Practice maximum rate and maximum angle climbing.		.7
20	Practice forced landings, steep turns and circuits.		.7
21	Demonstrate and practice crosswind takeoffs and landings, short takeoffs and short landings.	.4	

Lesson Number	Suggested Content	Suggested Time (hrs)	
		Dual	Solo
22	Practice crosswind takeoffs and landings, short takeoffs and short landings.		.7
23	Practice crosswind takeoffs and landings, short takeoffs and short landings.		.7
24	Check forced landings. Introduce low flying.	.5	
25	Practice low flying.		.7
26	**Exercises 10, 15 & 17.**		.7
27	**Exercises 10, 15 & 17.**		.7
28	Check all turns, stalling, circuits and various landings, forced landings and emergency procedures.	.8	
29	**Exercises 10, 12, 13, 15 & 17.**		.8
30	Revision of all exercises for flight tests.	.8	
31	Practice for flight test.		1.0
	TOTALS	**10.0**	**10.0**

Note: The above suggested syllabus does not include spinning or cross-country training. Additional time will be required to teach spinning, if it is authorized, and cross-country navigation.

Exercise 1
The Ultralight

Objective

To familiarize the student with the aircraft's controls and systems and teach him or her the checklists used for flying ultralights.

Considerations

The early impressions formed by students largely determine their attitude towards instruction and their confidence in themselves and the ultralight. The instructor must aim to develop the confidence and cooperation of his or her students from the outset. Students should not be swamped with a mass of detail at this stage.

Figure 1. A typical ultralight.

All the instruction in this exercise involving the external features of the ultralight, the cockpit layout and the checklists should be given at the aircraft. The instructor should first show the student the external features, pointing out constructional items such as control surfaces, landing gear details, fueling points, and so on.

Having dealt with the external points of primary interest, the cockpit can be entered and its layout explained. A good method of teaching the disposition of controls and instruments is to work through the checklists in the *Pilot's Notes*. In this way the student also learns to associate the Pilot's Notes with the aircraft.

The vital importance of systematic checking should be emphasized and the student should realize that checking every item on the checklist is essential to safe flying. Any questions should be answered within the limitations of the student's background knowledge.

Checklists

The student must learn all checklists thoroughly so that actions become instinctive. He or she should be able to locate all controls and switches without looking for them; to this end the student should sit in the cockpit and go through the checks with the aid of the Pilot's Notes.

Figure 2. View of cockpit.

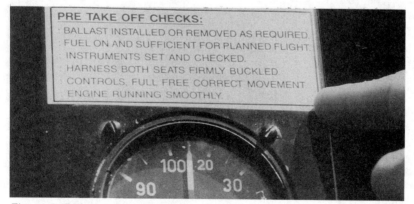

Figure 3. Before-takeoff checklist.

Emergency Procedures

When teaching the emergency procedures, emphasize that seconds will count if an emergency arises. Do not give the impression that such emergencies are commonplace. Stress the fact that, since emergencies are rare, the unexpected nature of the occurrence demands an instinctive reaction which needs to be performed at intervals. This will ensure that no time is lost through momentary confusion and indecision. The procedures for *fire* must be learned thoroughly.

Exercise 2
Before and After Flight

Objective

To teach preparation for flight and action after flight.

Considerations

Preparation for Flight

Flight Clothing

Most ultralight cockpits are open and the importance of wearing warm non-flammable clothing must be impressed upon students. Check their clothing to see that it fits correctly, otherwise discomfort may affect their flying.

Flight Authorization and Aircraft Acceptance

The use of the aircraft Maintenance Release and the Sign-Up Book should be explained and the student should be shown how to complete the documents before and after flight. At this early stage students should not be overburdened with preflight planning details, and only the more important points such as weather and the condition of the airfield state should be mentioned.

Figure.4. A well-dressed ultralight pilot.

External Checks

The instructor should point out the siting of the ultralight for starting, state of the ground, direction of slipstream, and so on; and the importance of checking the immediate taxi path for obstacles which cannot be seen from the cockpit.

Then the external check is carried out as detailed in the Pilot's Notes (see figure 6).

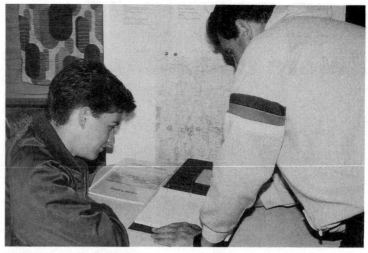

Figure 5. Filling out the Sign-Up Book.

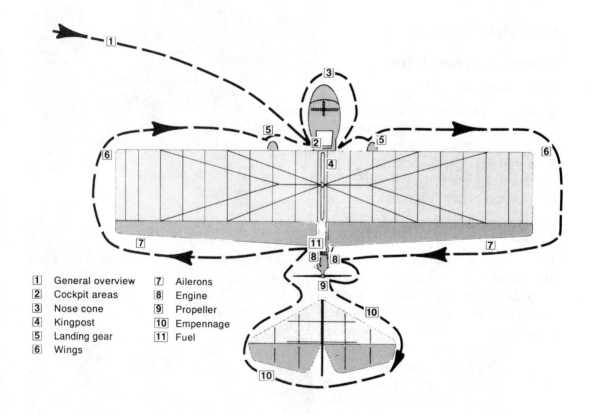

1	General overview	7	Ailerons
2	Cockpit areas	8	Engine
3	Nose cone	9	Propeller
4	Kingpost	10	Empennage
5	Landing gear	11	Fuel
6	Wings		

Figure 6. A typical "walk-around" pattern for the external check.

Internal Checks

On entering the cockpit, check that the student knows how to fasten and adjust the safety harness. After these preliminaries the internal checks, as listed in the Pilot's Notes, should be done. During these checks the student should be kept actively engaged; this not only helps him or her to learn the checks but makes him or her more familiar with the cockpit.

Figure 7. Completing the internal checks.

Starting and Warming-Up

During the warm-up period the student should be kept aware of the instrument readings and alert to the general nature of things going on in the immediate vicinity of the aircraft.

Power Check

The ultralight should normally be headed upwind and the control column held fully back to ensure that there is no risk of nosing over during the power check.

Action after Flight

Switching Off

Carry out the stopping procedure detailed in the Pilot's Notes. Tell the student about the danger associated with a "live" propeller if the ignition switches are left on.

Leaving the Aircraft

After vacating the cockpit carry out a final, brief external check of the ultralight and explain that this is done to check for any signs of leaking fluid or other indications of unserviceability. Ensure that the wheels are chocked before releasing the brakes, and that the aircraft is tied down if necessary.

Completion of the Sign-Up Book

Make certain that the student knows how to record his or her flying times in the Sign-up Book and the method of reporting defects.

Post-Flight Discussion

Students cannot be expected to remember all the detail involved in this exercise until they have had frequent practice. They should be supervised and checked as unobtrusively as possible, until proficient.

Exercise 3
First Flight

Objective

To introduce the student to the sensations of flying and the totally different aspect of the ground when seen from the air.

Figure 8. First flight.

Considerations

No detailed flying instruction should be given during the exercise, but this does not detract from its potential usefulness. During the flight the instructor can make his initial assessment of the student's in-flight temperament and decide on a tentative approach for subsequent instruction. The student becomes familiar with the aircraft and its operation by watching the instructor, and also becomes accustomed to the new environment and the novel sensations associated with flight.

The flight should be made in the vicinity of the airfield and local flying area so that local landmarks can be pointed out. After the student has settled down and is taking an active interest, his or her attention can be drawn to items such as the altitude and airspeed and the importance of the horizon as a visual aid to flying.

If the student shows signs of becoming airsick the flight should be discontinued, and if he or she is sick do not reveal any annoyance or show undue concern, but make light of the incident and assure him or her that sickness is not uncommon in the early stages.

The flight is for the benefit of the student and not a pleasure trip for the instructor. The impressions of the first flight can have a definite bearing on the student's subsequent interest, enthusiasm and ability to learn.

Exercise 4
The Controls

Objective

To teach the effects of moving the controls on the aircraft in flight.

Considerations

General

Since this exercise will be introduced during the student's first lesson in the air the instruction should be unhurried. Points which are obvious to the experienced pilot are not so obvious to the student and should not be glossed over or omitted. An example is the direction of movement of the aileron control and rudder pedals to obtain a required response from the aircraft. The student's clear understanding of the principles of this lesson is an essential foundation for later exercises. Usually more than one lesson is required to cover the scope of the exercise adequately.

The power settings and speeds given in this exercise should not be taught to the student, but are recommended to help the instructor to give satisfactory demonstrations. They are stated in general terms which are applicable to all three-axis ultralights.

Preparatory Theory

The following points should be discussed before the lesson. The subject matter should be confined to that of immediate interest:
- the function of the flight controls;
- the effects of airspeed and slipstream;
- the effect of banking the aircraft;
- the effect of yawing the aircraft;
- effects of power.

During Flight

Make certain that the student can hear clearly and is relaxed and comfortable. Check that he or she holds the controls correctly. Show how the horizon is used as a reference for interpreting the aircraft's attitude.

Avoid harsh control movements which may startle or cause discomfort to the student.

Allow the student to attempt all the effects demonstrated and give sufficient time for him or her to become used to the feel of the controls and to appreciate their effects.

Primary Effects of Controls

When showing the primary effects of the rudder, remind the student that the prime function of the rudder is not to control direction but to balance the aircraft in flight.

Show that the response of the ultralight to control movements depends on the airspeed and the amount of slipstream as well as on the quickness and magnitude of the control movements.

Secondary Effects of Controls

It must be quite evident to the student that only the one control is being used. This can be done by allowing the student to rest his or her hands and feet on the control during your demonstration.

Effect of Airspeed

Although the effectiveness of the controls is reduced and the airplane's response becomes less when the speed is reduced, positive control is still available.

Airmanship

Since the student cannot be expected to keep a good lookout at this stage, the instructor should explain the reason for any actions that he or she takes for reasons of good airmanship. Ensure that the student knows the correct method of handing over and taking over control.

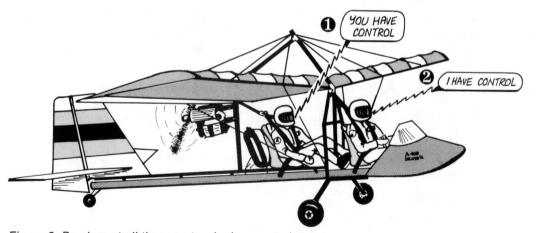

Figure 9. Be clear at all times as to who has control.

Air Exercise 4 **The Controls**

Skill 1: **Operate the elevators in straight-and-level flight at normal cruise speed.**

Technique	Observations
• Fore-and-aft movement of the control column.	Nose up and down—pitching; if a higher pitch attitude is held, airspeed reduces (and vice versa).

Skill 2: **Operate the ailerons in straight-and-level flight at normal cruise speed.**

Technique	Observations
• Lateral movement of the control column.	Wings up and down—rolling; Note initial *adverse yaw* as the ailerons are applied. If the ailerons remain applied, the aircraft will eventually enter a spiral descent.

Skill 3: **Operate the rudder in straight-and-level flight at normal cruise speed.**

Technique	Observations
• Rudder pedal movement.	Nose moves left and right—yawing; If the rudder remains applied, the aircraft can roll and will eventually enter a spiral descent.

Note: The main function of the rudder is to permit the pilot to fly the aircraft without yawing—that is, in coordinated flight.

(continued)

Skill 4: **Fly at low and high airspeed, with a constant power setting.**

Technique	Observations
Low Airspeed	
● Pitch the aircraft to a nose attitude slightly higher than that required for level flight so that the speed stabilizes comfortably just above the stall.	Less resistance to control movement and reduced effectiveness of all flight controls at low speed.
High Airspeed	
● Pitch the aircraft to a nose attitude slightly lower than that required for level flight so that the speed stabilizes comfortably just below the maximum permitted.	High resistance to control movement and increased effectiveness of all flight controls at high speed.

Skill 5: **Operate the throttle between idle and maximum power in flight.**

Low Power	
● While cruising in straight-and-level flight, move the throttle to *Idle*.	An immediate tendency for pitch and yaw changes. Decreasing rpm. Reduced effectiveness of the flight controls in the (now reduced) slipstream. Decreasing airspeed. Eventual descent.
High Power	
● While cruising straight-and-level, move the throttle to *Maximum Power*.	An immediate tendency for pitch and yaw changes. Increasing rpm. Increased effectiveness of the flight controls in the (now increased) slipstream. Increasing airspeed. Eventually, a climb.

Post-Flight Discussion

The Post-Flight Discussion should be a review of the Air Exercise.

Exercise 5
Taxiing

Objective

To teach how to move the aircraft safely on the ground.

Figure 10.

Considerations

General

The elements of taxiing should be introduced as early as possible. The student should be given progressively more responsibility as his or her proficiency increases. The temptation to take over control in order to save time must be resisted so that the student accumulates the maximum amount of taxiing experience under supervision.

The sequence in which the items of this exercise are taught depends on variables such as wind, airfield layout, and local regulations, as well as on the student's ability. The lesson should therefore be adapted to the prevailing circumstances. Whenever permissible the initial taxiing lessons are best done in an open space on the airfield where there is plenty of room to taxi about and practice.

Preparatory Theory

The following points should be discussed with the student before the lesson is commenced:

- the effect of inertia;
- use of controls;
- use of power;
- effect of wind;
- use of the brakes;
- engine handling.

During The Exercise

Emphasize the need for a constant lookout and the inherent lack of mobility of aircraft on the ground. Mention the following points:

- the flight controls have only indirect effects on steering of the aeroplane;
- the distribution of the keel surfaces tends to make the ultralight weathercock into the wind;
- there is a time lag between opening the throttle and the aircraft responding;
- tailwheel landing gear limits the turning ability of the aircraft owing to the effect of inertia.

Brake Failure

The main considerations affecting the action to be taken if the brakes fail are:

- proximity of obstacles and other aircraft;
- wind strength and direction;
- nature and slope of the surface.

All these points should be discussed with the student but it should be made clear that the safest course of action is to usually switch off the engine.

Look Out

The forward view from ultralights is generally good, however, the great importance of a continuous watch for obstacles and other traffic should be emphasized. When taxiing, pilots must be prepared to give way to aircraft approaching to land and taking off.

Starting and Stopping

More power is required to start the aircraft moving than to keep it moving because of the higher initial power needed to overcome the inertia of the stationary aeroplane. Throttle movements and brake applications should always be smoothly executed and the control column held back while doing so. Harsh braking, excessive use of power, and failure to keep the control column back can cause the ultralight to nose over. To stop normally, first close the throttle and then, if necessary, apply the brakes.

Control of Speed

When demonstrating the correct taxiing speed, point out that the most accurate assessment is obtained from observing the movement of the ground close to the aircraft. Before applying the brakes, close the throttle.

Directional Control and Turning

The method of controlling direction is through the use of the steerable nose or tail wheel and the rudder. Power is used only to increase the slipstream over the rudder (to increase rudder effectiveness) in cases when the extra power will not result in an excessive taxiing speed. The direction and amount of control movement required to enter and leave a turn must be anticipated. These are affected by the wind velocity, and whether the turn is made into the wind or downwind.

Starting to Taxi

Immediately the ultralight moves forward the throttle should be closed and the brakes applied to test their effectiveness.

Taxiing in Strong Winds

Normally the control column is held fully back while taxiing. If the wind is strong and blowing from behind, the control column should be held central or forward to prevent the wind from blowing against the under surface of the elevators and lifting the tail. The tendency to weathercock may be overcome by a combination of rudder and use of aileron, aiming to keep the upwind wing down (see figure 11).

Airmanship

The student should be told that the pilot-in-command is ultimately responsible for the safety of the aircraft and that he or she needs to keep a very good lookout while taxiing.

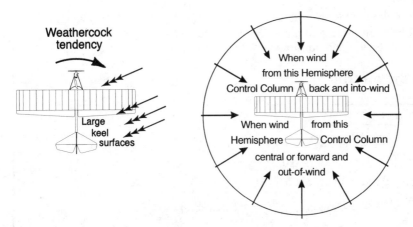

Figure 11. There is a tendency to weathercock into the wind.

Air Exercise 5 **Taxiing**

Skill 1: Commence taxiing.

Technique

- Close the throttle, and remove the chocks if they are in place.
- Ensure that the intended taxiing path is clear (and do not cut corners).
- Hold the control column back and apply sufficient power to get the aircraft moving.
- Check the brakes as soon as possible by throttling back and applying them gently.
- Check the instruments when clear of the parking area.

Skill 2: Taxi the aircraft.

Technique

- Control the direction by using the steerable nosewheel or tailwheel through the rudder pedals.
- The radius of turn depends upon the amount of rudder pedal used.

Observations

- Only a moderate radius of turn can be achieved.
- A need to anticipate corners.
- Tendency to *weathercock* (that is, turn into the wind).
- Turns into the wind tend to tighten up.
- Airplane is more difficult to turn when taxiing downwind.
- Control **speed** with *power* and *brake* (but do not use power against brakes).
- Ideal taxiing speed is a fast walking pace.
- Requirement for use of power or brakes is affected by ground slope, nature of the surface, and the wind.

Skill 3: Stop the aircraft.

Technique

- Close the throttle.
- Centralize the rudder pedals.
- Smoothly apply the brakes.

Note: There is no "Post-flight Discussion" for this Exercise

Exercise 6
Straight-and-Level

Objective

To teach how to fly the ultralight accurately straight-and-level.

Considerations

General

Accurate straight-and-level flight is required for certain types of operation; therefore, the student should be ultimately required to attain a high standard.

Figure 12. The horizon in straight-and-level flight.

Preparatory Theory

You should discuss with the student the effect of turbulence and vertical air currents on a slow, low-inertia aircraft.

During Flight

Straight-and-Level Flight at Cruising Power

Pay attention to the following points:

- The student should concentrate initially on judging the aircraft attitude by the position of the horizon and then use that attitude to fly straight-and-level.
- The student should be shown how to choose a reference point on which to keep straight and how to bring the aircraft back to that point if the direction alters.
- Errors in the altitude and airspeed should be corrected by making a number of small adjustments to the pitch attitude. This is to avoid the common error of "chasing the needles".

A marked unbalance in the ultralight can be detected in two ways:

- the sensation of yaw can be felt, and;
- when the wings are level, the yaw can be seen.

A slight unbalance in the ultralight is more difficult to detect.

After the student has become fairly proficient at maintaining straight and level flight the instructor can introduce disturbances by upsetting the aircraft's attitude and then asking the student to restore it to the original situation.

Straight-and-Level at Various Airspeeds

- While flying at a constant attitude, an increase in airspeed using power causes the ultralight to climb; a decrease causes it to descend. The correct technique, therefore, is to readjust the attitude as the airspeed changes.
- The correction for the yaw which occurs during a power or airspeed change is a point that requires careful instruction.

Airmanship

Again emphasize the importance of a good lookout. Introduce the *clock* system of reporting traffic sightings and ask the student to report the position of other aircraft by using this system.

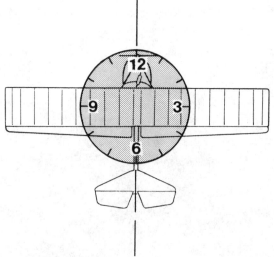

Figure 13. The clock code.

Air Exercise 6 **Straight-and-Level**

Skill 1: **To fly the aircraft in straight-and-level flight with cruise power set.**

Technique and Observations

- Maintain the wings level with respect to the horizon by using the ailerons, and keep the aircraft balanced using the rudder.
- Select and hold a pitch attitude with respect to the horizon.
- Select a feature in the distance toward which you are flying.
- Check the **altitude**. If the aircraft has descended, reselect a slightly higher pitch attitude (and vice versa if the aircraft has climbed).
- Check the **direction** by seeing if you are still flying toward the distant feature originally selected. If the aircraft has deviated from straight-and-level flight, then re-level the wings, re-establish coordination, and then make a gentle turn back the distant feature.
- Note that accurate straight-and-level flight requires the coordinated use of the controls to ensure that the aircraft remains level in altitude and straight in direction.

Skill 2: **To decelerate and fly the ultralight in straight-and-level flight at slow speed.**

Technique and Observations

- While in straight-and-level flight, partially close the throttle to reduce power.
- Note that the aircraft loses speed and begins to descend.
- As the speed reduces, raise the nose sufficiently to maintain level flight.
- When the aircraft has stabilized, note the new pitch attitude and airspeed.

CAUTION
The aircraft cannot maintain altitude if the power is reduced too much, because the wings will eventually stall.

(continued)

Skill 3: Accelerate and fly the ultralight in straight-and-level flight at high speed.

Technique and Observations

- While in straight-and-level flight, open the throttle to increase power.
- Note that the airspeed increases and the aircraft commences to climb.
- As the the speed increases, lower the nose sufficiently to maintain level flight.
- When the aircraft has stabilized, note the new pitch attitude and airspeed.

CAUTION
Monitor the airspeed constantly to ensure that the maximum allowable airspeed is not exceeded.

Post-Flight Discussion

Difficulties encountered in eliminating yaw are often due to the aircraft wings not being level when attempting to balance the aircraft.

Exercise 7
Climbing

Objective

To teach how to climb the ultralight at a desired airspeed between two altitudes.

Considerations

General

Usually an ultralight climbs at the airspeed recommended in the Pilot's Notes—this speed giving the best compromise between maximum rate of climb, engine handling and mobility.

Preparatory Theory

The following points should be known by the student before you begin the lesson:

- effect of changing power;
- recommended airspeeds;
- engine limitations;
- effect of altitude;
- effect of turbulence.

During Flight

The Normal Climb

During a climb the student should be taught to hold the selected climb attitude for sufficiently long enough to enable the airspeed to stabilize before making any adjustments to the pitch attitude.

Leveling Off

Until a student is proficient at leveling off from the climb he or she should not be expected to level off at a precise altitude. In the early stages students encounter difficulty in leveling off correctly and maintaining a constant altitude at the same time. The difficulty is often caused through the progressive attitude change required as the airspeed increases.

Maximum Rate of Climb

The best rate of climb is achieved at the airspeed which realizes the greatest excess of power over that required for straight-and-level flight and is stated usually in the Pilot's Notes. The rate of climb decreases as altitude increases.

Airmanship

A good lookout should cover the whole area around the airplane, but during the climb the area into which the airplane is moving is especially important.

Engine performance should be checked periodically.

Air Exercise 7 **Climbing**

Skill 1: Enter a climb from straight-and-level flight.

Technique and Observations

- Ensure that the path above is clear.
- Increase power to climb power, and prevent yaw with rudder.
- Simultaneously, raise the nose to the climb attitude, and hold it.
- Ensure that the wings are level with the horizon and that the aircraft is coordinated.

Skill 2: Climb the ultralight normally on a constant heading.

Technique and Observations

- Maintain a constant heading using the same technique described in straight-and-level.
- Control the airspeed by varying the pitch attitude—if the airspeed is too low, then lower the nose slightly (and vice versa).
- Monitor the engine for smooth and correct operation.

Note: For maximum rate of climb, or for best climb angle, a higher pitch attitude and a lower airspeed is required.

Skill 3: Level off from a climb and resume straight-and-level flight

Technique and Observations

- Anticipate the level-off altitude.
- Gradually lower the nose to the straight-and-level attitude as the aircraft accelerates to normal cruise speed.
- reduce power to cruise power—prevent yaw.

Post-Fight Discussion

The student often fails to correct for yaw after changing power. The student must be taught to anticipate this, and use rudder pressure to keep the aircraft coordinated.

The student should be reminded of the importance of monitoring engine performance.

Exercise 8
Descending

Objective

1. To teach how to descend the ultralight at a desired airspeed between two altitudes.

2. To teach the student, by use of sideslipping, how to increase the rate and angle of descent with no increase in forward speed.

Considerations

General

An accurately controlled and coordinated descent involves two variables which must be correctly related to obtain the required conditions for the descent. The variables are airspeed and power.

Since these variables assume added importance on the approach to land, it may be advisable to review this exercise before teaching landings.

The instructor must only demonstrate the sideslip when it is permitted on the aircraft and can be used to advantage.

Preparatory Theory

You should ensure that the student considers:

- the effect of power;
- recommended airspeeds;
- engine limitations;
- effect of wind and windshear;
- sideslipping;
- effect of high drag;
- effect of turbulence.

During Flight

The Glide

The glide can be established in two ways:

- Throttle back and immediately assume the glide attitude, allowing the speed to stabilize in its own time, or;
- Throttle back and delay assuming the glide attitude until the speed approaches the desired gliding speed, then lower the nose to the glide attitude. The glide is established more quickly by using this method.

The student may encounter some difficulty in judging the glide attitude. However, the instructor must persevere until the student can determine the correct attitude quickly and clearly. As early as practicable the student should be made to cross refer to the instruments. Airspeed in the descent can be increased by lowering the pitch attitude with the elevator and, conversely, can be decreased by raising the pitch attitude.

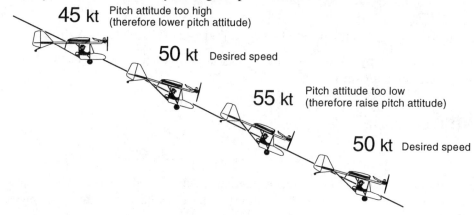

Figure 14. Control the descent airspeed with pitch attitude.

Effects of Power

To ensure that the student becomes proficient at descending under defined conditions he or she should be given frequent practice at varying the power while maintaining constant airspeed. The greater the power, the shallower the descent.

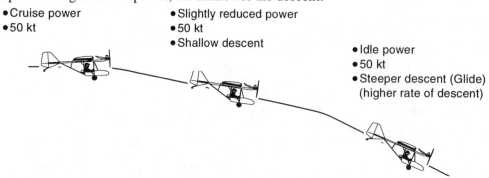

Figure 15. Control the rate of descent with power.

Cruise Descent

It should be pointed out that the cruise descent is the normal method of losing altitude, because it is comfortable and less stressful on the engine.

The Sideslip

The sideslip is an out-of-balance operation with bank applied one way and rudder applied the other. If approved for the aircraft, it can be used to steepen the descent angle (by increasing the rate of descent for a given airspeed).

While the student is learning how to use the controls during a sideslip, the exercise should be performed at altitude. Subsequent practice can be near the ground at a forced landing field or airfield.

The student should be shown and become convinced of the effect of sideslipping on the relationship between heading and ground path. This can be done by sideslipping along a straight road or some similar line feature on the ground.

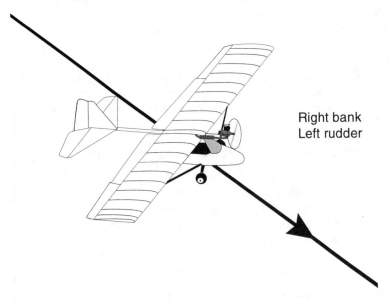

Right bank
Left rudder

Figure 16. A sideslip to the right.

Airmanship

During a *long descent* the heading should be changed at intervals so that a lookout can be maintained in the area into which the aircraft is descending. Power should also be applied from time to time to keep the engine warm and the spark plugs clear of fouling.

When sideslipping, a *safe* airspeed must be maintained. This particularly applies during the recovery.

Air Exercise 8 **Descending**

Skill 1: Enter a straight descent from straight-and-level flight.

- Ensure that the path below is clear.
- Reduce power to *Idle*, prevent yaw.
- Simultaneously, lower the nose to the glide attitude and hold it.
- Ensure that the wings are level with the horizon, and that the aircraft is coordinated.

Skill 2: Descend the aircraft normally on a constant heading.

- Maintain a constant heading using the same technique used for flying in straight-and-level.
- Control the airspeed by varying the pitch attitude—if the airspeed is too low, then lower the nose slightly (and vice versa).
- Monitor the engine for smooth and correct operation.

Note: As the power is gradually increased above idle, the nose must be raised to maintain the same airspeed (and vice versa if the power is again reduced). As power is increased the rate of descent will decrease if the same airspeed is held. *Power* and *attitude* can thus be varied to control the descent path.

Skill 3: Level off from a descent and resume straight-and-level flight.

- Anticipate the level-off altitude.
- Simultaneously raise the nose to the straight-and-level attitude and increase the power to cruise power—prevent yaw with rudder.
- Resume straight-and-level flight.

Skill 4: Sideslip the airplane during a glide descent.

- Check that it is approved to sideslip the machine.
- To enter a sideslip, simultaneously apply rudder and opposite bank.
- Control the *rate of descent* with bank.
- Control *direction* and *rate of turn* with rudder; note the angle between heading and ground track.
- Control the airspeed with pitch attitude.
- To recover from a sideslip, centralize the controls and resume a glide descent.

Post-Flight Discussion

Common Errors

The student does not allow enough time for the airspeed to stabilize and consequently chases the airspeed needle.

When sideslipping, students often apply too much rudder for the utilized bank angle. Explain that only a certain amount of rudder should be used in relation to a certain bank angle of bank.

When recovering from a sideslip there is a tendency to lose airspeed. Emphasize the need to lower the nose to maintain the normal gliding speed.

Exercise 9
Turning

Objective

To teach how to turn to a specified heading using a medium bank angle.

Considerations

General

For the purposes of this exercise, the amount of bank used should not exceed 30°. Turns using higher angles of bank are considered to be steep turns.

All medium turns should be taught before starting traffic patterns.

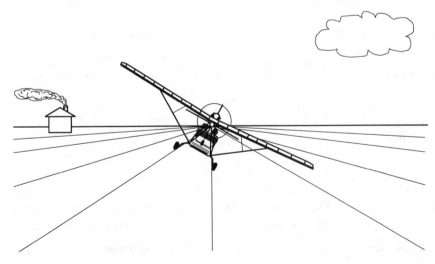

Figure 17. A 30° turn to the right.

Preparatory Theory

The student should have covered the following theory before the lesson:

- principles of turning;
- use of controls when turning;
- use of power;
- climbing and descending turns.

During Flight

The initial emphasis should be placed on the correct judgment of attitude and angle of bank through the use of the horizon as an external reference.

The student should be able to enter and leave turns smoothly before progressing to sustained turns through large changes of heading.

| LEVEL | A MEDIUM RIGHT TURN | A STEEP RIGHT TURN |

Figure 18. The view from the cockpit.

The direction of turn should be alternated so that the student obtains practice in turning in both directions.

The student should be taught to be systematic and apply the following basic checks to all turns:

- look out;
- bank angle and coordination;
- attitude and speed.

Level Turns

In an accurate level turn the airspeed settles at a slightly lower figure than in straight flight at the same power. Once the aircraft is in a steady turn, the airspeed should not fluctuate.

The seating arrangement in ultralights can make it difficult for the student to judge the attitude, but a little practice will solve this problem.

Climbing Turns

The handling technique is the same as for level turns, but the speed is adjusted and maintained by varying the pitch attitude. The bank angle should be limited to avoid a substantial reduction in the rate of climb.

Descending Turns

The handling technique for entry and recovery is the same as for climbing turns, but the nose must be lowered slightly when entering a descending turn to maintain the airspeed.

The effects of power are the same as for a straight descent.

At this stage the student should be told that high angles of bank increase both the rate of descent and the stall speed; and that more power, a higher airspeed, or a combination of both, can be used as a safeguard when necessary.

Airmanship

The student often forgets to maintain a good lookout while concentrating on flying accurately. He or she should be told that a good lookout is very important before and during a change of direction, particularly on the side toward which he or she is turning. During the exercise students should be required to orient themselves at intervals so as to develop a sense of direction.

Air Exercise 9 **Turning**

Skill 1: **Make a level turn at a medium bank angle (30° or less) using cruise power.**

Technique and Observations

- Observe the airspeed before entry.
- Look out to ensure that the way is clear.
- To **enter** the turn, coordinate the use of ailerons and rudder to roll smoothly to about the correct angle of bank, maintaining pitch attitude with elevator.
- To **maintain** the turn, hold the correct angle of bank and pitch attitude. Observe altitude, rate of turn, and heading using aircraft instruments and external features. If the aircraft climbs, lower the nose slightly (and vice versa). Continue to look out to ensure that the way is clear. Note the airspeed.
- To **exit** the turn, anticipate the heading change during rollout. Coordinate the use of aileron and rudder to roll smoothly to wings level. Maintain pitch attitude using elevator. Resume flying straight-and-level. Observe airspeed.

Skill 2: **Make a climbing turn (at 15° bank angle) using climb power.**

Technique and Observations

- Observe the rate of climb and airspeed before entry.
- Look out to ensure that the way is clear.
- To **enter** the turn, coordinate the use of ailerons and rudder to roll smoothly to about the correct angle of bank, maintaining airspeed by adjusting pitch attitude with elevator.
- To **maintain** the turn, hold the correct angle of bank and pitch attitude. Observe airspeed, rate of turn, and heading using aircraft instruments and external features. If the airspeed is too low, lower the nose slightly (and vice versa). Continue to look out to ensure that the way is clear. Observe the rate of climb.
- To **exit** the turn, anticipate the heading change during rollout. Coordinate the use of aileron and rudder to roll smoothly to wings level. Maintain the climb airspeed by adjusting pitch attitude with elevator. Resume the straight climb and again note the rate of climb.

(continued)

Skill 3: Make a descending turn (30° angle of bank) using idle power.

Technique and Observations

- Observe rate of descent and airspeed before entry.
- Look out to ensure that the way is clear.
- To **enter** the turn, coordinate the use of aileron and rudder to roll smoothly to about the correct angle of bank, maintaining airspeed by adjusting the pitch attitude with elevator.
- To **maintain** the turn, maintain the correct angle of bank and pitch attitude. Observe the airspeed, rate of turn, and heading using the instruments and external features. If the airspeed is too low, lower the nose slightly (and vice versa). Continue to look out to ensure that the way is clear. Observe the rate of descent.
- To **exit** the turn, anticipate the heading change during rollout. Coordinate the use of aileron and rudder to roll smoothly to wings level. Maintain airspeed by adjusting the pitch attitude with elevator. Resume the straight descent and note the rate of descent.

Skill 4: Make a powered descending turn (30° angle of bank) using less than cruise power.

- As for a normal descending turn, except that the rate of descent is reduced by using some power.

Post-Flight Discussion

Most faults stem from the lack of proper coordination of the controls. It should be made clear to the student that a correction to any one of the variables involved in a turn will require adjustments of the others. Proficiency can be improved by getting the student to maintain altitude and aircraft coordination while banking from/to port and starboard.

Faulty turns often result from inaccurate flying just before entering the turns.

Some students become confused about the function of the controls when the aircraft is banked. It should be made clear that the controls still retain their basic functions when the aircraft is banked — that is, the ailerons control the angle of bank, the elevators control the pitch attitude, and the rudder controls yaw.

Students often fail to maintain an adequate lookout in the direction of the turn during sustained turns.

Exercise 10
Stalling and Slow Flight

Objective

To teach how to recognize an approaching stall and how to recover with the minimum loss of altitude.

Considerations

General

The ultimate aim of this exercise is to teach the student how to recover from a stall with the minimum loss of altitude; however this aspect should not be over-emphasized in the early stages of the exercise. The student should first be able to identify the symptoms of a stall and know the correct method of recovery under all circumstances.

Preparatory Theory

Prior to flight you should discuss:
- lift, the stall angle of attack and the stall speed;
- characteristics of the stall;
- factors affecting the stall speed;
- altitude and the stall;
- recovery from the stall—use of power.

During Flight

The student may be a little nervous at first; this is understandable, but he or she will gain confidence when able to identify and recover from the stall. As soon as possible the student should be allowed to stall the aircraft and recover, and should be given plenty of practice until he or she becomes thoroughly proficient and confident.

In the early stages watch for symptoms of air sickness and discontinue the exercise if necessary.

Principal emphasis must be placed on the recognition of stall warnings and the stall recovery. Although a practical method of entry must be taught, it is of less importance. If the ultralight drops a wing at the stall, the observations dealing with this additional consideration should be brought in from the start. Stalling in turns is considered under steep turns.

The First Stall

The student's first experience of a stall should show that it is not in any way a frightening experience and should rid him or her of any false ideas of danger and violent sensations. The first stall is best done at the end of the lesson preceding that on which stalling is to be dealt with in detail. No instruction should be given during the first demonstration but the point of stall and the commencement of recovery should be indicated. During the subsequent post-flight discussion the stall, as demonstrated, should be covered and the student's questions answered. In this way the student is prepared better for the detailed lesson on stalling.

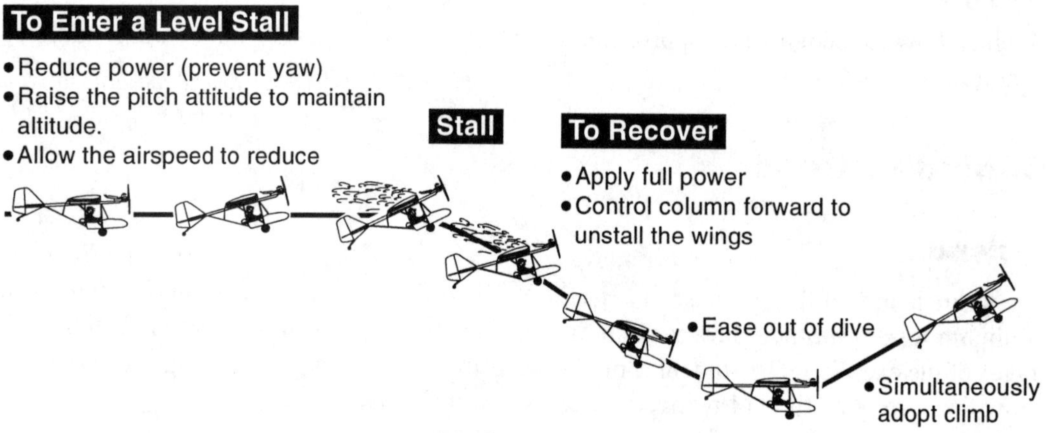

To Enter a Level Stall

- Reduce power (prevent yaw)
- Raise the pitch attitude to maintain altitude.
- Allow the airspeed to reduce

Stall

To Recover

- Apply full power
- Control column forward to unstall the wings
- Ease out of dive
- Simultaneously adopt climb

Figure 19. The stall and the stall recovery.

Symptoms of the Stall

A high nose-up attitude of the aircraft is not always a fundamental symptom of an approaching stall. Stalling of the wings occurs when the critical angle of attack is exceeded, and the airflow over the wings becomes turbulent. It can occur in any attitude if the aircraft is mishandled. The nose-up attitude should only be pointed out when it is a valid indication that a stall is imminent.

Students must be given plenty of practice at *approaching* the stall and detecting the symptoms for themselves. They should become thoroughly familiar with the stall-warning symptoms of the ultralight.

Effect of Power on Recovery

The significantly smaller amount of altitude lost during the stall by using power in the recovery should be emphasized.

Recovery when the Wing Drops

The student should be told that the use of aileron will not always raise a dropped wing and may aggravate the situation under certain conditions. Therefore, because of this possibility, ailerons are not used in the recovery, until the wings are unstalled.

Recovery from the Incipient Stall

An unintentional stall should always be stopped at the incipient stage; therefore, the emphasis should be placed on quick recovery action as soon as any impending stall symptoms are recognized. The student should be given ample practice in recovering from the incipient stage of all types of stalls.

Stall under Approach Configuration

The demonstration should be made as realistic as possible. Show how lack of attention to accurate flying can lead to a stall when concentrating on the approach to land.

Stall at Higher Speeds

Students should be under no doubt that the aircraft can be stalled at any speed and power. They should understand that the more extreme cases cannot be demonstrated because of the possibility of overstressing the aircraft.

Effect of Power on the Stall

Show the pupil that, when the ultralight is stalled with power on, recovery from the incipient stage can be made by simply releasing the backward pressure on the control column. It should be made quite clear that this applies only at the incipient stage and not when the full stall has occurred.

Airmanship

Before carrying out stalling practice, ensure that:
- altitude is sufficient to recover by 1500 feet AGL;
- harness is locked and tight;
- not over a built-up area;
- look out—check all clear.

Air Exercise 10
Stalling and Slow Flight

Skill 1: Enter a stall from straight-and-level flight.

Technique	Observations
• Close the throttle– prevent yaw	Airspeed reduces.
• Raise the nose as the airspeed reduces, to maintain altitude.	Controls are less effective.
	High pitch attitude just before the point of stall.
	Nose drop at the point of stall.
	Possible wing drop.
	Descent.

Skill 2: Unstall the airplane without using power.

Technique	Observations
• Move the control column forward sufficiently to unstall the wings.	
• If a wing has dropped, apply opposite rudder to prevent further yaw.	Full control has now been regained.
• Level the wings with aileron.	
• Ease out of the dive.	Note the amount of altitude lost.

CAUTION

If the "easing out of the dive" is too sudden, the aircraft may restall at a higher speed. Recovery from such a stall is immediate upon releasing some of the back pressure on the control column.

(continued)

Skill 3: **Unstall the airplane, using power to minimize the altitude loss.**

Technique	Observations
• Simultaneously apply full power and move the control column forward sufficiently to unstall the wings. • If the wing has dropped, apply opposite rudder to prevent further yaw. • When control is regained, level the wings using aileron. • Ease out of the dive. • Adopt a climb attitude with climb power set.	Considerably less altitude is lost when power is used in the recovery.

CAUTION

If the throttle is opened too rapidly the engine may cut out.

Skill 4: **Recover from an incipient stall.**

- Just prior to the point of stall, apply full power.
- Prevent yaw.
- Maintain pitch attitude.
- Note the small altitude loss as the ultralight commences to accelerate.

Skill 5: **Enter a stall with some power applied, and then recover.**

- Technique is the same as for stalling without using power, except that the throttle is partially opened.
- The airspeed reduces less rapidly.
- The flight controls that are in the propeller slipstream remain more responsive than the flight controls that are out of the slipstream (for example the ailerons).
- The stall occurs at a slightly lower airspeed.
- The stall is more marked and a wing is more likely to drop. The recovery is faster because some power is already applied.
- The overall altitude loss is less.

(continued)

Air Exercise 10 (continued)

Skill 6: Enter a stall from an approach configuration and recover.

Technique	Observations
• Simulate (at altitude for safety reasons) a base turn.	
• Raise the nose to about the "cruise" pitch attitude.	The airspeed reduces.
	Controls become less effective.
	At the point of stall apply the stall recovery technique, using power to reduce altitude loss.

> **CAUTION**
> In a stall from a turn, a large wing drop is possible if the inner wing drops.

Post-flight Discussion

Students often have difficulty in estimating the amount of control column movement required to recover from the stall. Frequent practice and advice from the instructor is needed until the student becomes proficient. When the instructor is demonstrating the recovery, the student should be allowed to rest his or her hands and feet on the controls.

Students must appreciate how far the nose should be lowered to unstall the aircraft. They should realize that if the nose is lowered too far then a greater amount of altitude will be lost, but if it is not lowered far enough the ultralight may not unstall, or may stall again.

When a wing drops at the stall, the student tends to correct by instinctive use of aileron. Only by practice and experience can the proper method of using rudder to prevent further yaw be learned. Students must realize however that, if a wing drops, ailerons should be used to level the wings as soon as they are unstalled. They must understand that only a little back pressure should be applied until the wings are level.

When power is applied during recovery, the throttle movement by the student is often hesitant or slow. If this is so, the student should be told that the amount of altitude lost and the rapidity with which control is regained both depend on the prompt use of high power.

Students initially have difficulty in judging the dive recovery. They usually tend to either re-stall the aircraft or recover too slowly. They should be shown how the rate of recovery is dependent on the airspeed available.

Exercise 11
Spinning

Objective

To teach how to enter, maintain and recover from a fully developed spin.

WARNING

Most ultralights are not certified for aerobatic flight, and cannot be used for spinning.

Considerations

General

Although it is not unusual for students to be somewhat nervous during their first few spins there may be some doubt as to their suitability for further training if they continue to be fearful.

Practice spins, dual and solo, should be done at intervals throughout the student's training, but only from altitudes which allow sufficient room for safe recovery.

Spinning is the most frequent cause of airsickness and the lesson should be discontinued if signs of illness appear.

Preparatory Theory

The following matters should be discussed with the student before teaching spinning:

- causes, stages and characteristics of spins;
- recovery action;
- engine handling.

During Flight

The differences between spins and spirals should be made clear. Spirals are recognized by a rapid increase in airspeed. Spins usually settle after four to five turns when the speed begins to stabilize, rotation becomes constant, the spinning attitude flattens and control forces required to hold the aircraft in the spin become less.

The Student's First Spin

The considerations are the same as those for the student's first stall and the spin should therefore be done at the end of the lesson before that on which spinning is to be taught. This first spin should consist of not more than two or three turns. Before entry, put the student at ease and ask him or her to tell you the direction of rotation. Do not do any other instruction.

Spin Entry from Level Flight

To enter a spiral, bring the aircraft towards the stall, and just before the stall apply rudder in the direction required to spin.

To enter a spin, begin applying pro-spin rudder as the airplane is approaching the stall and allow the aircraft to stall with the nose only slightly above the horizon. At the stall apply full rudder, full back stick and full opposite aileron. Until the spin stabilizes the controls must be kept fully applied.

Recovery from Spins

The same recovery action is to be taught for the recovery from spins and spirals, but in the case of the spiral, the recovery is instantaneously effected when pro-spin control pressures are removed.

The student should be warned that higher control column forces are required to recover from the spin, and the aircraft may take several turns to stop spinning. When recovering from prolonged spins, the student should locate the horizon and use it as a datum for leveling the wings. If the student experiences any dizziness advise him or her that such dizziness is not unusual.

Recovery at the Incipient Stage

When the student has mastered the recovery from the fully developed spin, the emphasis should be placed on early recognition of the various conditions that can lead to a spin and recovery at the incipient stage. An unintentional spin is usually the result of an uncorrected or undetected stall, but in most cases the warning symptoms are so clear that the impending spin can be recognized and corrected before it reaches an advanced stage.

The incipient spin recovery action introduces a new technique. The student should be told that it does not replace the standard spin recovery action which must be used in a fully developed spin. He or she needs to know where the incipient stage of the spin ends and the fully developed spin begins. This demands accurate and skillful instruction.

Testing the Student's Recovery Techniques

When the student has mastered the incipient spin recovery, he or she should be tested through the full range of recovery techniques from the incipient stage of the stall to the fully developed spin. The aim should be to clear away any confusion in the student's mind by ensuring he or she comprehends the differences between each recovery action.

Spin from a Level Turn

Enter a level turn with low power and tighten the turn until the aircraft spins.

Spin from a Gliding Turn

The student should be shown how it is possible to spin from gliding turns through misuse of the controls to maintain the turn. The direction of spin is not necessarily the same as the turn, as it depends on the way the controls are misused. For example, the aircraft may be turning left with left aileron applied, but by misuse of the controls (say by holding the nose up and not correcting right yaw) the right wing may stall causing the aircraft to enter a spin to the right.

Airmanship

To avoid the chance of any misunderstanding during spin recovery, the words "recover now" should always be used when telling the student to recover. The student should acknowledge with "recovering now" when he or she starts the recovery.

When a spin is recognized, recovery should be initiated so that it will be completed before maximum allowable airspeed is reached, otherwise the airframe will be overstressed.

Air Exercise 11 **Spinning**

Skill 1: Enter a spin from straight-and-level flight.

Technique	Observations
• Initially use the technique required to enter a stall from straight-and-level flight.	The aircraft must stall before it can spin.
• At the point of stall, simultaneously move the control column fully backwards, apply full pro-spin rudder and full opposite aileron.	The aircraft will begin to 'auto-rotate'.
• Maintain full pro-spin controls until wanting to recover.	After about two turns the pitch attitude flattens out, the speed stabilizes and the rate of rotation stabilizes.

Skill 2: Recover from the spin at the incipient phase (before the spin stabilizes).

Technique

- Centralize the controls.
- Close the throttle.
- When the spin stops, look for the horizon and level the wings.
- Ease out of the dive and apply power as required.

Observations

- Advantage of taking recovery action at the incipient stage.
- Importance of being quick and positive.

CAUTION

If the aircraft does not respond to the incipient spin recovery action, then the full spin recovery action must be used.

(continued)

Air Exercise 11 (continued)

Technique and Observations

Skill 3: Recover from a fully developed spin.

- Throttle closed.
- Centralize controls.
- Full opposite rudder.
- Control column steadily forward until the spin stops.
- Centralize the controls.
- Level the wings.
- Ease out of the dive.
- Apply power and enter a climb.
- Note the altitude loss.

Post-Flight Discussion

Many students forget to throttle back after entering a spin from a flight condition in which power was being used.

The student often attempts to identify the behavior of the ultralight from the position of the controls. It should be impressed on him or her that the position of the controls is not a reliable indication of whether a spin has occurred or the nature of the spin. The spin should be identified from:

- the flight conditions immediately before the suspected spin—that is, the proximity to the stall, the amount of yaw, nose down, or if in a spiral descent—some, or all, of these characteristics will be evident;
- the attitude of the aircraft, loading and characteristics of the spinning motion;
- a high rate of descent, with the airspeed building up or remaining steady at a low figure.

Students are often unprepared for the high elevator forces encountered in the recovery from a stable spin, and therefore do not apply sufficient forward stick, or are too slow in doing so.

Exercise 12
The Standard Takeoff and Climb to Downwind Leg

Objective

To teach how to take off and climb into the traffic pattern to the downwind leg.

Considerations

General

Before first solo, the student should be able to carry out an upwind takeoff and should have practiced the procedure to be used following engine failure after takeoff. Use of a Two-Way radio should be discussed.

Preparatory Theory

The student should understand the following, before being taught to takeoff:

- the use of elevators and rudder;
- the effects of crosswind;
- the use of power;
- engine failure procedure;
- drills and traffic pattern procedure;
- factors affecting length of ground run;
- use of a two-way radio.

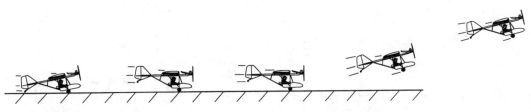

Figure 20. The takeoff

During Flight

Takeoff into the Wind

If the student has difficulty when attempting to takeoff unassisted, it may be necessary to let him or her use each control in turn, the instructor handling the others. As the student gains proficiency, he or she should be allowed to take over the other controls until the complete takeoff can be carried out unassisted.

Whenever possible the demonstrations and practice should be made flying into the wind.

The student should select a distant reference point ahead on which to keep straight during the takeoff.

Crosswind Takeoff

The tendency to weathercock is controlled by the use of rudder. In addition it may be necessary to use aileron to prevent the upwind wing from rising. On the ground:

- keep straight with rudder; and
- keep the wings level with aileron.

After leaving the ground, the student should be required to counteract for any wind drift so as to make good a track along the extended takeoff direction.

If the crosswind is not strong enough for a convincing demonstration, the lesson should be postponed until better conditions are available.

Engine Failure after Takeoff

This demonstration should be made from an altitude and position which allows time for the instructor to make all necessary observations and give full effect to the lesson. Make certain that no other aircraft are below.

Most ultralights will decelerate very quickly toward the stall after an engine failure in the climb unless the nose is lowered to the gliding attitude. **Students must comprehend the need to lower the nose as soon as a power failure is detected.**

It should be pointed out that most ultralights will lose at least 200 feet in a 180-degree gliding turn. As a general rule, it is unwise to attempt to turn back to the airfield in the event that the engine fails shortly after takeoff.

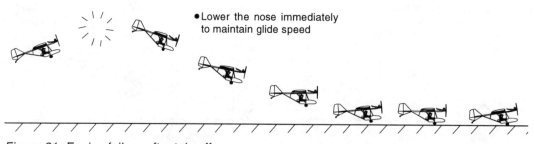

Figure 21. Engine failure after takeoff.

It should be emphasized that the actions in the event of an engine failure after takeoff should be considered before takeoff.

If the engine fails during the takeoff or when the ultralight is just airborne, the procedure is governed by the overall situation. A landing (if airborne) should be made, and the three-point attitude (if the tail is off the ground) should be resumed as quickly as possible before the brakes are used. Following an aborted takeoff it may also be necessary to turn sharply while on the ground to avoid striking obstacles.

Short Takeoff

The ultralight is flown off in the shortest possible distance. The subsequent climb may be as for a normal takeoff or at a maximum angle for obstacle clearance.

The sequence can be made more realistic by first explaining the practical applications, for example:

- flying from an advanced landing ground which has a limited length of run;
- flying from an airfield of marginal size in light or zero-wind conditions;
- flying from an airfield of marginal size with obstacles at the upwind end.

In general, the power should be increased to the maximum that can be held on the brakes before starting the takeoff run.

Airmanship

The paramount importance of a good lookout must be stressed and a high standard demanded.

The student must be taught to make a thorough check of the vital actions, in the correct sequence. The instructor must insist on accuracy and attention to detail in this matter and the student must be fully aware of the importance of these checks.

Impress upon the student the need to note the direction and strength of the wind before and after lining up for takeoff.

Air Exercise 12 **The Standard Takeoff and Climb to Downwind**

Technique and Observations

Skill 1: Takeoff the aircraft.

Lining Up

- Line up in the intended direction of takeoff, ensuring the tail/nose wheel is straight before stopping.
- Select a significant feature in the distance directly ahead of the aircraft to use as a reference point during the takeoff.
- Ensure all 'Before Takeoff Checks' are completed.

The Takeoff Run

- Hold the control column back and, if there is a crosswind, into the wind as well.
- Advance the throttle slowly to maximum power and ensure the engine is operating normally.
- Use the rudder to control any tendency for the aircraft to change direction.
- As the airspeed increases, ease forward on the control column to lower the nose (tailwheel aircraft only).

Note: For a "short takeoff" maximum power should be achieved before the brakes are released—otherwise power can be applied while the aircraft is rolling.

CAUTION
If the engine fails to operate normally during the takeoff run:
- close the throttle;
- keep straight with rudder;
- use the brakes to stop;
- switch off the ignition.

(continued)

Technique and Observations

Skill 2: Handle an engine failure after takeoff .

- Lower the nose immediately to maintain glide speed. Choose a landing area within an arc of approximately 30° either side of heading, preferably upwind.
- Close the throttle.
- Fuel off, if applicable.
- Ignition off.
- Land the aircraft.

Skill 3: Position the aircraft on the downwind leg of the traffic pattern after takeoff:

- At about 250 ft, commence a climbing turn to the "crosswind" leg.
- At about 500 ft, level off to the cruise and then turn to the "downwind" leg.

Notes

1. In crosswind conditions the time taken on the "crosswind leg" can vary and it might be necessary to commence a turn to the "downwind leg" before 500 ft is reached. When on the "downwind leg", allow for drift to achieve a ground track that is parallel to the runway. Select a distant ground feature as a reference point to aim at.

2. The height used by ultralights in traffic patterns will vary depending on local airfield requirements. The heights used in this manual assure that the traffic pattern downwind is 500 feet above ground level.

Post-Flight Discussion

Overcontrolling and lack of coordination are usually caused by muscular tenseness on the controls brought about by the high amount of concentration required in the initial attempts. The student can be helped to relax if his or her responsibility is at first limited.

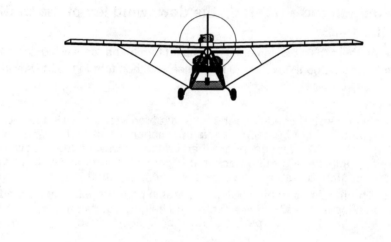

Exercise 13
Airport Traffic Patterns, Approaches and Landings

Objective

To teach how to fly the various traffic patterns and how to land the ultralight.

Considerations

General

Before the first solo flight the student should be able to make competent engine-assisted approaches and landings and also be able to go around again safely. Power-off approaches and landings should also have been carried out sufficiently for the student to be able to attempt a landing in the event of engine failure.

Preparatory Theory

Before teaching airport traffic patterns, the student should have considered:

- rejoining procedures (see figure 22);
- the pattern, approach and landing;
- use of brakes;
- effect of crosswind;
- going around again;
- considerations for short landings.

Note: The traffic pattern described in this manual is indicative only. Traffic patterns actually flown must comply with rules and regulations applicable to the airport being used.

Pattern rejoining procedures

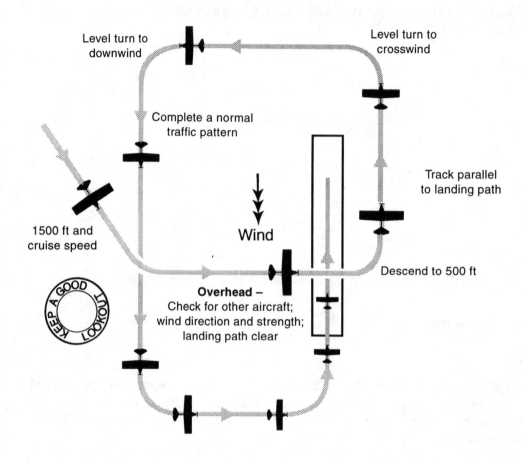

Level turn to
downwind

Level turn to
crosswind

Complete a normal
traffic pattern

Track parallel
to landing path

Wind

1500 ft and
cruise speed

Descend to 500 ft

Overhead –
Check for other aircraft;
wind direction and strength;
landing path clear

Figure 22. Pattern rejoining procedures.

During Flight

Many students have difficulty in mastering the landing and, although the instructor's advice and guidance is of help, proficiency is attained mainly through practice. In the early stages, the emphasis should be placed on safe flying and fostering of the student's confidence, rather than a polished performance. Although some students may have no difficulty with the landing, it is important to ensure, before the first solo, that they can recognize and correct any errors that may occur.

Engine-Assisted Approach and Landing

The engine-assisted approach and landing is the basic technique, and all others are variations of it. When on base leg, the student should be told to look for other aircraft that are making their final approach.

The importance of flying an accurate traffic pattern and approach should be emphasized. The cause of a bad landing can often be traced to a poor approach, which in turn was caused by a poor traffic pattern.

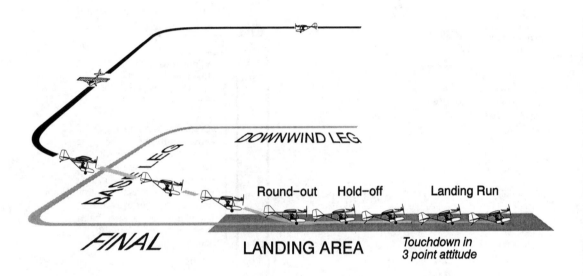

Figure 23a. Approach and three-pointer landing.

Balked Approach

Stress the importance of a very good lookout during the initial stages of the go-around.

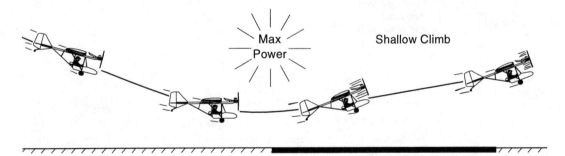

Figure 23b. The balked approach.

Normal traffic pattern

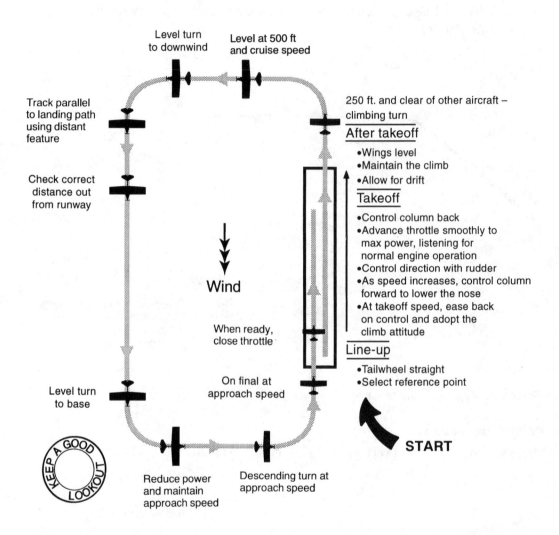

Figure 24. The normal airport traffic pattern.

Level turn to downwind

Level at 500 ft and cruise speed

Track parallel to landing path using distant feature

Check correct distance out from runway

Wind

250 ft. and clear of other aircraft – climbing turn

After takeoff
- Wings level
- Maintain the climb
- Allow for drift

Takeoff
- Control column back
- Advance throttle smoothly to max power, listening for normal engine operation
- Control direction with rudder
- As speed increases, control column forward to lower the nose
- At takeoff speed, ease back on control and adopt the climb attitude

When ready, close throttle

Line-up
- Tailwheel straight
- Select reference point

Level turn to base

On final at approach speed

START

KEEP A GOOD LOOKOUT

Reduce power and maintain approach speed

Descending turn at approach speed

The Glide Approach and Landing

If the airspeed is allowed to fall below the recommended approach speed at the start of the round-out, the rate of sink can become so high that a heavy landing may be unavoidable. Any attempt to check the high rate of descent by a correspondingly large movement of the control column can aggravate the situation.

Glide approach

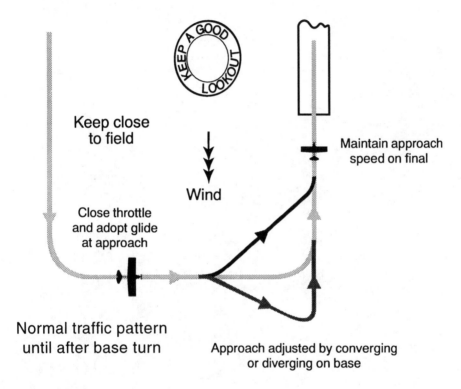

Figure 25. The glide approach.

Short Landing

Since the aircraft can sink sharply when the throttle is closed, it is important that this is done only when it is correctly positioned for the touchdown.

The landing run should be shortened by the application of as much brake as possible once the aircraft is firmly on the ground. The student should be warned of the dangers of excessive braking on a tailwheel-equipped ultralight.

Airmanship

Because other aircraft may be in the pattern a very high standard of lookout must be demanded.

Check wind strength and direction before joining the traffic pattern.

Ultralights are extremely sensitive to turbulent air and great care should be exercised in the pattern where mechanical and/or thermal turbulence is present.

Turns in the pattern should be normally limited to medium angles of bank (30 degrees).

Air Exercise 13 **Traffic Patterns, Approaches and Landings**

Technique and Observations

Skill 1: Fly the "downwind" leg.

- Maintain straight-and-level flight at 500 feet.
- Ensure the aircraft is the correct distance from the landing path.
- Accomplish any "Before Landing Checks" which have to be done.
- Look for the correct place to turn to "Base Leg", and look out for other aircraft in the pattern, and ensure the runway is clear.

Skill 2: Fly the "base" and "final" legs.

- Make turn from downwind to base.
- Reduce power for descent.
- Enter the descent.
- Alter power to correct any undershoot/overshoot.
- Maintain descent speed until commencing the round-out.
- Look for point at which to commence "round-out".

Note: Adjust the pitch attitude to control airspeed; adjust power to control rate of descent.

Skill 3: Land the aircraft.

1. The Flare or Round-out

- Apply judgment to recognize when to commence the round-out.
- Close the throttle to *Idle* power.
- Gradually raise the nose attitude so that the descent is converted to decelerating level flight just above the landing path.
- If the nose is raised too quickly the ultralight will "balloon", and if raised too slowly it will strike the ground prematurely.

Note: As the airspeed reduces, increased back pressure will be required on the control column to prevent the nose from dropping.

> ### CAUTION
> If the round-out point is too high the aircraft may stall before it can be landed, and if it is too low it may strike the ground prematurely.

2. Touchdown

- When the correct landing attitude has been obtained, allow the aircraft to sink onto the ground.

Note: The landing attitude will be somewhat higher for a "three-point" landing than for a "wheeler" landing.

(continued)

Technique and Observations

3. Landing Run

- As the ultralight decelerates, gradually ease the control column back, keeping the wings level with aileron.
- Keep straight with rudder.
- Apply the brakes to stop.

Note: For a "touch-and-go", the takeoff is usually commenced when the ultralight is on three wheels in the landing run.

- Open the throttle to maximum power and prevent yaw.
- Raise the tail as the throttle is opened (tail wheeled aircraft).
- Lift off at takeoff speed.

Skill 4: Fly a balked approach.

If, while on final, a decision is made to abort the landing:

- Open throttle smoothly to maximum power and prevent yaw.
- Simultaneously commence a shallow climb-away.
- Ease onto the non-active side of the runway to avoid other aircraft if necessary.

Skill 5: Fly a glide approach and landing.

- Fly a normal traffic pattern until after the turn to "base leg" is completed. Initially plan to touch down one-third of the way down the landing strip.
- When within gliding distance of the planned touchdown point, close the throttle. Note the steep angle of approach and high rate of descent.
- Make whatever corrections you need to the approach path to achieve a safe touchdown by converging or diverging while on base leg.
- Maintain the glide until the round-out point is reached.

CAUTION
The round-out point should be slightly higher than that for a normal landing because of the larger pitch change required in the flare.
Avoid making a high hold-off.

(continued)

Technique and Observations

Skill 6: Fly a short landing.

- Base leg as for normal powered approach.
- Speed regulated with power.
- Pre-selected touchdown point.
- Speed progressively reduced to recommended speed.
- Commence round-out at the runway threshold with power on.
- Immediate touchdown when throttle is closed.
- Use of brakes to stop.

Skill 7: Crosswind Traffic Patterns.

- Allow for drift if it is encountered in the pattern by altering the heading of the aircraft slightly into the wind.
- Just before touchdown, use the rudder pedals to align the aircraft with the landing path, keeping the wings level with aileron.
- Maintain some upwind aileron during the landing roll.

Post-Flight Discussion

The usual causes of bad landings are:

- Insufficient round-out from too steep an approach—can be caused by an early tendency to overshoot.

- Starting to round out correctly and then failing to either adopt or hold the landing attitude. This is caused by the student not looking far enough ahead. The correct three-point attitude should be pointed out while taxiing.

- Holding off too high. This is sometimes caused by fear of getting too near the ground. The fault can often be cured by a clear demonstration of the hold-off height done by flying the ultralight along the airfield in the appropriate attitude and at the correct hold-off height.

- Erratic bad judgment of the hold-off height and poor control of direction during the hold-off; this is usually caused by looking at the ground too close to the aircraft and becoming tense on the controls.

- Not keeping the wings level. This is also often caused by looking at the ground too close to the aircraft.

- General difficulty with all stages of the landing up to the touchdown. This trouble can be traced to:
  - faulty approaches with airspeed too high or too low;
  - fluctuating approach speed and over correcting with the throttle.
- Poor control of direction during the landing run. Possible causes are:
  - relaxing concentration after touching down;
  - over-controlling with the rudder and brakes, due to tenseness on the controls;
  - failure to choose a reference point on which to keep straight;
  - too many consecutive touch-and-go landings have been made so that the student lacks practice of controlling the landing run.

Landing errors are likely to be of a random nature while students are becoming accustomed to the appearance and feeling of a good landing. After the student has grasped the basic requirements, errors will normally form a consistent pattern which can be easily recognized and analyzed.

During the initial period when students are feeling their way, the instructor should help by demonstrating landings when necessary and then guiding and advising during students' attempts.

Exercise 14
First Solo

Considerations

The first-solo flight is an important occasion, as both the student and instructor must try to ensure that the student starts the flight with the knowledge that he or she is fully competent to fly solo. A successful first-solo flight, free from incident, gives the student added confidence which is often apparent as an improvement in overall flying skill.

One of the main problems in flight instruction is the recognizing and selecting the right moment to send students on their first-solo flight. In the one extreme, if they are sent solo before they are sufficiently confident and competent, the result may be a poor flight and a loss of confidence. In the other extreme, if the first solo is delayed until after the appropriate moment, the result is usually a deterioration in their standard of flying and a loss of interest.

The main requirement is not for polished flying but for general competence and safety and the ability to correct faults. The instructor must be sure that the student can take the appropriate measures promptly in an emergency. To this end the student's reaction should have been noted at times when anything in the nature of an emergency has occurred in training flights.

Students should be tested orally for knowledge of FAR Part 103 Operating Regulations concerning ultralight aircraft. No student should be allowed to fly solo without demonstrating adequate knowledge of those operating rules.

A guide to what constitutes an acceptable standard of flying for the first-solo flight is given below.

Takeoff and Climb

The student should be able to safely correct imminent swings on takeoff. He or she should fly the aircraft off and climb at a safe speed and not hold it on the ground until too high a speed is reached.

The Traffic Pattern

Although their flying need not be precise in all respects, students should be capable of flying a reasonably accurate pattern. Variations in altitude are acceptable provided that they are corrected; however, the variations should not be large enough to cause marked difficulty on the approach.

The Approach

The student should have a good control of the aircraft's airspeed, particularly during the final turn and in the last stages of the approach. He or she should be able to anticipate the need for corrections to the approach and the necessity for going around if the circumstances warrant it, that is these decisions should not be left until the last moment.

The Landing

The main consideration is whether the landings are safe. There should be no consistent faults such as holding off high. A series of good landings is not necessarily proof of readiness for solo unless the student has shown an ability to go around safely and is able to correct a bad landing.

Airmanship

The student should be capable of maintaining a good lookout without reminders from the instructor. All checks and emergency procedures should be faultless. There should be no doubt of his or her ability to avoid other aircraft and choose a safe landing path.

Figure 26.

Emergencies

The student must have had practice at handling simulated engine failures after takeoff. He or she should have a thorough knowledge of the actions to be taken in the event of fire in the air and on the ground.

Only a short briefing is necessary, and this can be given while the instructor is taxiing to the takeoff point. The student should be reminded of points such as special air traffic requirements, and crosswind conditions. No detailed instructions should be given other than the fact that he is to take off, complete the traffic pattern, and land. If possible traffic density should be low; airfield control (if present) should be told that the flight is a first solo.

The instructor can often gain useful information by watching the flight from the edge of the airfield.

Figure 27.

Exercise 15
Steep Turns

Objective

To teach how to fly a level steep turn.

Considerations

General

Steep turns give valuable practice in coordination of control movements and give the student confidence in handling the aircraft. The student should be given enough practice to reach a high standard.

Figure 28. Cockpit view of a steep turn.

During Flight

Level Steep Turns

Steep turns should first be made at an angle of bank of about 45°; as the student becomes proficient the bank can be increased to about 60°, depending on aircraft limitations.

Good practice in coordination can be obtained from turning in alternate directions and making the change in a smooth continuous movement.

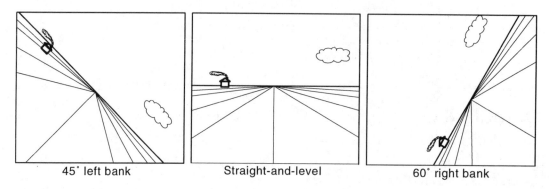

45° left bank   Straight-and-level   60° right bank

Figure 29. Steep turns—the view from the cockpit.

Stalling in the Turn

This lesson should have been thoroughly learned before the student does a solo practice involving steep turns.

Before demonstrating stalling in a turn, the student should be told what to expect when the ultralight stalls.

When recovering from a stall in a turn, power must be applied unless the nose is well below the horizon.

Airmanship

Emphasize the vital importance of keeping a good lookout when changing direction rapidly.

Students may become disoriented after a number of steep turns. They should be reminded of the importance of keeping a periodic check of their position.

Air Exercise 15 **Steep Turns**

Technique and Observations

Skill 1: Fly a steep turn.

Entry as for medium turn and then:
- Increase power slowly as bank is further increased.
- Progressively increase the back pressure on the control column to hold the pitch attitude as the bank exceeds 30°.

CAUTION

If too much back pressure is applied the aircraft may stall. To recover, simply relax some of the pressure on the control column.

In the Turn
- Control altitude by adjusting the bank angle — that is, if the airplane starts to descend, reduce the angle of bank, and vice versa.
- Maintain a good lookout.
- Note the high rate of turn.

Recovery
- Recovery is the same as for medium turns, except that power should be reduced when the cruising speed is regained.

Post-Flight Discussion

The student often fails to appreciate that, while the airplane is steeply banked, the use of the elevator to control the height also causes the turn to tighten. The student should be told to reduce the bank before attempting to raise the nose in an effort to correct unwanted descent.

Exercise 16
Flying At Low Level

Objective

To teach how to fly the ultralight near the ground with confidence and safety.

Considerations

General

Although the student should fly confidently and with the requisite amount of flair, the instructor should immediately curb any tendency toward overconfidence or disregard of regulations. Low flying requires a high standard of both flying ability and self-discipline. The student should be taught to approach this exercise with these points in mind.

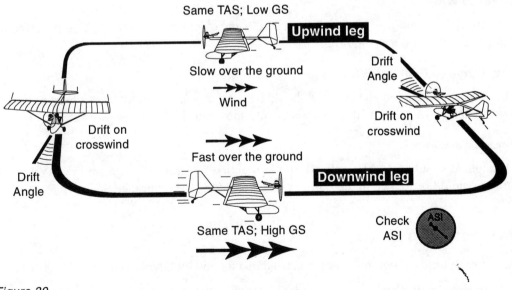

Figure 30.

Preparatory Theory

The following points should be discussed prior to the first low flying lesson:

- regulations;
- effect of wind;
- effect of rough air;
- effect of aircraft inertia;
- flying over sloping or otherwise uneven ground;
- effect of limited visibility on ground reference (horizon).

During Flight

In the early stages the lesson should not be too long because of the intense concentration required from the student. The length and difficulty of the task should be increased progressively.

Familiarization at Low Level

The first tasks should be simple and the student should be allowed to handle the controls as much as possible. Point out the danger of relying on the altimeter when close to the ground. The correct height above the ground should be demonstrated and the student told to pay particular attention to the appearance of the ground at that height.

Point out the necessity of anticipating changes in power when flying over marked contour changes. The position in the low-flying area should be checked frequently to avoid leaving the area unintentionally.

Effect of Wind

The low-flying patterns shown in figures 31a, b and c are valuable for teaching the effect of wind and the allowances required.

Low Flying in Poor Visibility

The first demonstration and practice should be done in good visibility. Later lessons can be given in lesser visibility, with emphasis on attitude control.

Forced Landings

The student should be proficient and safe in practice forced landings from low level. Such failures should be treated in the same way as engine failures after takeoff.

Airmanship

Accurate flying is important near the ground and a good lookout is essential.

The student should check the wind strength and direction before commencing low flying.

Low Flying Pattern A

The ground reference point is on the intersection of two straight-line features crossing at 90°. Fly along one and complete a figure of eight so that it remains central over the point of intersection.

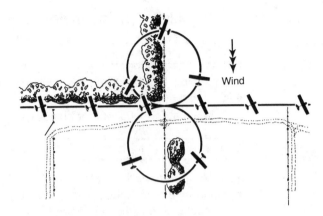

Figure 31a.

Low Flying Pattern B

The ground reference point consists of two prominent features (for example, tall trees) situated sufficiently near to each other for both to be always visible, but not so near as to necessitate continuous turns.

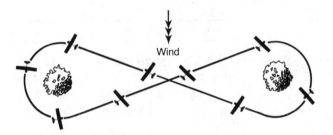

Figure 31b.

Low Flying Pattern C

Use the same ground reference point as for 'A'. The pattern consists of a figure-of-eight in which the straight leg of each line feature follows each turn.

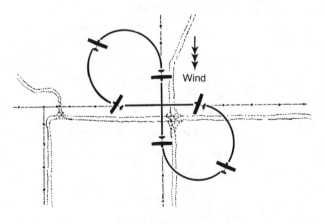

Figure 31c.

Air Exercise 16 **Flying at Low Level**

Skill 1: Descend into the low-flying area.

Technique

- Descend into a low-flying area using a cruise descent.
- Assess the wind direction and strength.
- Maintain a good lookout for obstacles.

Observations

- Moderate rate of descent.
- Importance of lookout.
- Increasing impression of speed.
- Changing aspect of ground features.

Skill 2: Fly at low level.

Technique and Observations

- Maintain a good lookout to avoid obstacles.
- Fly about 100 feet AGL at cruise speed.
- Use power as required to maintain altitude over sloping ground.

Note: The altimeter is of little use in assessing or maintaining 100 feet AGL.

- Drift more apparent than at altitude.
- The low ground speed when flying upwind (and vice versa) is very apparent.
- Drift gives the impression of a slip or skid in turns.

CAUTION

- Avoid the tendency to fly lower when flying upwind.
- Allow for drift when avoiding obstacles.
- Avoid terrain which rises more sharply than the ultralight can climb.
- Avoid over-tightening turns to compensate for drift.

Post-Flight Discussion

The post-flight discussion should be a full review of the Air Exercise.

Exercise 17
Forced Landings

Objective

1. To teach how to make a safe approach and landing after partial or complete engine failure.

2. To teach how to make an emergency landing in a field when power is available, say due to stress of weather.

Considerations

General

The student should demonstrate a satisfactory ability to carry out this exercise before leaving the airport traffic patterns on solo flight.

Preparatory Theory

The following points must be discussed with the student prior to the Air Exercise:

- forced landing procedure;
- factors governing the choice of a landing area;
- actions after landing.

During Flight

The exercise is best taught in two stages:

- The instructor does the various cockpit checks while the student concentrates on flying the ultralight and planning the descent.
- The student flies the complete exercise—both flying and completing the checks.

The student should be given dual and solo practice at forced landings at intervals throughout his or her training.

When the student reaches a suitable standard at the basic exercise, the practice can be made more realistic by the instructor closing the throttle without warning at various altitudes and under different conditions. The student should say which field he or she has chosen so that the instructor can assess the procedure.

Choice of Field

From altitude it is difficult to assess the nature of the ground surface. Therefore, until the ultralight is low enough for the pilot to make an accurate assessment, the aircraft should be guided toward an area that seems to be generally suitable.

For the demonstration the instructor should choose a field which can be identified easily by the student.

Figure 32. Heading toward a suitable area.

The Initial Descent

Stress the importance of flying the aircraft accurately in the glide while planning. Point out that the descent should be planned to arrive at the glide base position.

The altitude at the time of the emergency greatly influences the plan of action. Broadly, the lower the altitude, the more the plan of action should approximate to that for an engine failure after takeoff. Many factors may affect the course of action and some of these are listed for discussion with the student:

- altitude above the ground;
- position of suitable fields;
- wind strength and direction;
- weather;
- whether the engine has failed partially or completely;
- level of pilot experience.

Checks

When the student is sufficiently competent at forced landings he or she should be required to give the forced landing checks verbally on every practice.

Final Approach

It is not necessary to continue the approach to almost ground level, as the success or failure of the practice forced landing can be gauged from a safer altitude.

The amount of field taken up by the round-out and float should be demonstrated on the airfield. Occasional practice forced landings should be made on the airfield.

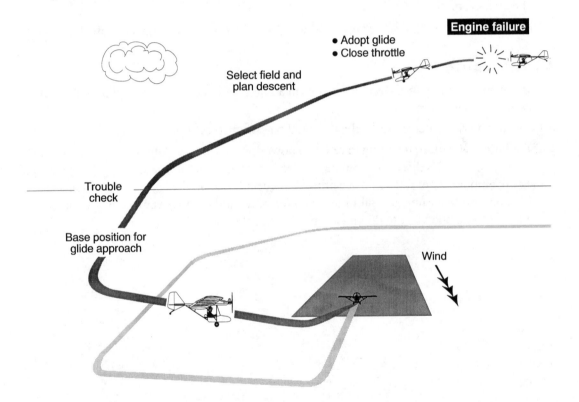

Figure 33. Example of a forced landing.

Forced Landings with Power (Precautionary Search and Landing)

A forced landing is sometimes necessary for reasons other than engine failure. Such landings can be due to pilot error and poor airmanship, typical causes being:

- poor navigation (lost);
- deteriorating or poor weather conditions.

In other cases the forced landing may be unavoidable for reasons out of the pilot's control.

The following list of factors all have a bearing on the forced landing with power and should be discussed with the student:

- If possible locate an airfield for the landing. If the airfield is disused it should be checked for suitability since many disused airfields have obstructed landing runs.
- The landing should be made before the fuel is exhausted—enough fuel should be kept in reserve to allow for locating, checking and landing before the tanks have run dry.
- The field should be selected using the same principles as those used for a forced landing—the approach path and landing run can be inspected at low altitude.
- If conditions allow, a normal pattern should be made and the short landing procedure used if the area is small.
- If it is difficult to keep the selected field in sight, a low-level pattern can be made.

Airmanship

The decision to switch off the engine or not (in a real emergency) is governed largely by the following two considerations:

- If the engine has failed completely, it should be switched off immediately.
- If the failure is partial, resulting in reduced power or intermittent running, the engine may be used at the pilot's discretion, but he should remember that the windmilling engine may pick up temporarily or fail again at a critical stage and so spoil the approach. In such a case it may be best to assume a total failure and not rely on the faulty engine. However, only the pilot can decide what to do under a particular set of conditions.

Air Exercise 17 **Forced Landings**

Technique and Observations

Skill 1: Land the aircraft after experiencing an engine failure.

Immediate Actions
- Lower the nose and adopt the glide altitude.
- Close the throttle.
- Check for fire.

Select a Place to Land

Assess:
- Wind strength and direction.
- Size and shape.
- Surface.
- Obstacles—undershoot and overshoot.
- Slope.
- Approximate elevation of field.

Plan Descent

Take into account:
- Wind strength.
- Altitude available.
- Traffic pattern direction.

Trouble Check

Conduct the "trouble check" detailed in the 'Pilot Notes'.

If Unable to Restart Engine
- Continuously review the plan.
- Turn off the ignition, battery and fuel.
- Tighten the seat belts.
- Land using the glide-approach technique on base and final.

Post-Flight Discussion

Students often encounter difficulties when learning forced landings because they tend to rush or attempt to perform too many checks during the limited time available. Emphasis must be placed on flying the aircraft safely down onto the ground.

Exercise 18
Pilot Navigation

Objective

To teach the student how to fly cross-country with visual reference to the ground.

Considerations

General

The student should have been introduced to the following aspects of navigation during general flying training:

- the use of large features for orientation;
- the use of the magnetic compass;
- map orientation;
- simple map reading;
- estimation of distances, bearings and headings;
- FAR Part 103 Regulations pertaining to standard operation of ultralights: hazardous operations, daylight operations, right-of-way, operations over congested areas, operations in class A,B, C or D airspace, visual reference with surface, flight visibility and cloud clearance requirement.

Preparatory Theory

Students should have covered, in detail, the following theory:

- meteorological forecasts;
- chart preparation;
- flight planning calculations and use of the flight computer;
- methods of correcting the heading;
- air traffic regulations (FAR Part 103);
- procedure when lost;
- diversions;
- range and endurance flying. (Ultralights are limited to carrying 5 US gal)

Before Flight

Students should be helped with the preparation of their flight plans for the first navigation exercise. Their working of the computer should be checked, and they should be helped with map preparation and advised on the choice of check points and positions for obtaining bearings. Any other aids available for the exercise should be discussed.

During Flight

CLEAR Checks

Students should be taught to learn the *CLEAR* checks and apply them at significant points in the flight. They comprise:

- **C**ompass—correct heading—make a common-sense heading check using large features.
- **L**og times and ETAs on chart.
- **E**ngine—power setting correct, sufficient fuel remaining.
- **A**ltimetry—mean sea level altimeter setting —correct altitude.
- **R**adio report (if relevant).

Setting Headings

Teach students to make a common-sense check of the general direction of flight by using knowledge of local features. This avoids the chance of making gross errors such as flying on reciprocal headings or setting the airspeed as a heading.

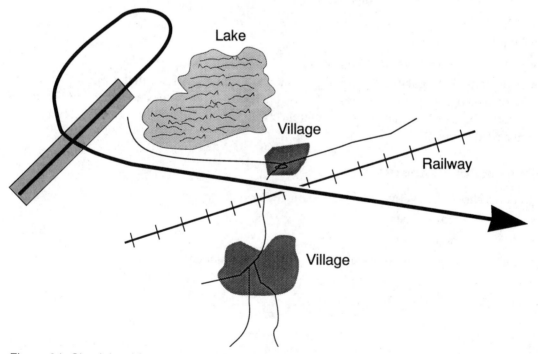

Figure 34. Check local features soon after setting course.

Chart Reading

The value and reliability of a pinpoint depends mostly on whether it is unique in relation to its surroundings. The value of certain types of pinpoints may change with seasons or weather conditions. For example, large industrial towns may be obscured by haze, or rivers and lakes may have dried up through lack of rain.

Furthermore, the appearances of features changes with altitude. At the lower altitudes, the vertical height and shape of a ground feature becomes more important than its appearance in plan. Small but unique features are often of greater use than large, more common ones. Features are more easily missed while at the lower altitudes because they are in view for only a short time, especially those near the planned course; the appearance of a feature must therefore be anticipated and, to this end, a careful preflight study of the chart is most important.

If a feature is missed, a search should not be made for it, but the flight continued and the next feature anticipated. However, if a series of features are missed the student must gain altitude and find his or her position. In choosing features for pinpoints the student should aim to include features which will indicate tracking error as well as timing error.

Students may often become confused by attempting to correlate an excessive amount of detail. They should be told to use only the major pinpoints in conjunction with the flight plan and calculations, and to avoid continuous map reading involving the location and identification of minor features. A good technique is to determine (roughly) the aircraft's position by dead reckoning, look for large features to ascertain your position generally on the chart and then refine the position by looking for more detailed information.

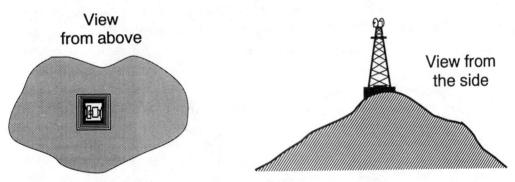

View from above

View from the side

Figure 35. The side elevation of features is important at low altitudes.

Navigation Work Cycle

Students should be taught to develop a "navigation work cycle", which they should complete midway between turning/reporting points or at about every twenty minutes.

The work cycle should involve:

- Ascertaining the aircraft's position.
- Checking the achieved track over the ground and, if necessary, determining a new heading to fly by using the "one-in-sixty" rule.

- Checking the groundspeed and, if necessary, revising the ETA for the next turning/reporting point.
- Carrying out the *CLEAR* checks.

Notes on the 1:60 Rule

- Tracking error in degrees, is calculated from the distance off course and the distance covered.
- The method is practicable over any distance.
- It can be used to fly parallel to planned course, to regain planned course and to fly direction to the destination.

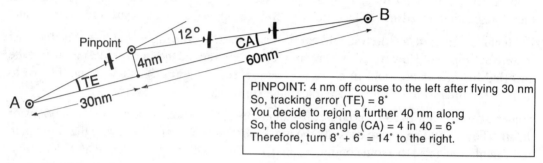

PINPOINT: 4 nm off course to the left after flying 30 nm
So, tracking error (TE) = 8°
You decide to rejoin a further 40 nm along
So, the closing angle (CA) = 4 in 40 = 6°
Therefore, turn 8° + 6° = 14° to the right.

Figure 36. The 1:60 rule.

Notes on Revising ETA

- Take an accurate time.
- Use the principle of proportions, for example, if the aircraft is one minute late after covering one-third of the distance, then add three minutes to the original ETA.
- Re-check timing at subsequent feature markers.

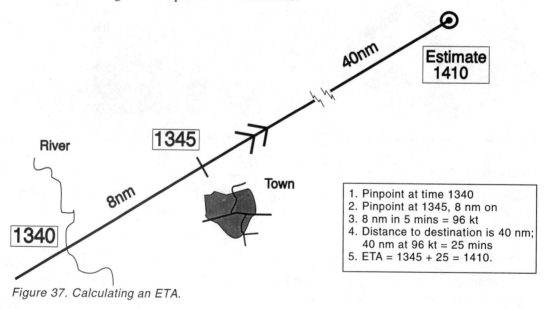

1. Pinpoint at time 1340
2. Pinpoint at 1345, 8 nm on
3. 8 nm in 5 mins = 96 kt
4. Distance to destination is 40 nm; 40 nm at 96 kt = 25 mins
5. ETA = 1345 + 25 = 1410.

Figure 37. Calculating an ETA.

Airmanship

Fuel awareness should be emphasized. Before flight a study of the weather, ATC requirements (including NOTAMs) and for the destination airfield is essential.

The student should not neglect to look out whilst engrossed in navigational matters; any laxity should be checked. Weather, engine instruments and ATC requirements must be monitored periodically en route.

The student must understand what to do if he or she becomes lost—that is, climb immediately, maintaining heading and visual flight conditions, until sufficient terrain can be seen to provide a definite pinpoint. If he or she is unable to orient position:

- estimate the fuel remaining;
- fly for endurance at a safe altitude;
- assess the situation and if still unable to determine position, find a safe place to land and seek advice.

Figure 38. Arriving safely at the destination.

Air Exercise 18 **Pilot Navigation**

Technique and Observations

Skill 1: Set the aircraft on course.

- After takeoff, turn in the traffic pattern direction, climb to the cruising altitude, and from overhead the airfield note departure time.
- Carry out a **CLEAR** check in the cruise:
  Compass—correct heading—common sense heading check using large features.
  Log times and ETAs on chart.
  Engine—power setting, fuel quantity sufficient.
  Altimetry—altimeter to MSL pressure—at correct altitude.
  Radio report (if relevant).

Skill 2: Navigate the aircraft in flight.

- Maintain accurate cruise altitude, heading and airspeed.
- Use the "navigational work cycle" midway between turning/reporting points, or at not more than twenty minute intervals.
- Do the *CLEAR* checks after each turning/reporting point.

Skill 3: Land at destination.

- When the destination is positively recognized, alter heading visually.
- Join the traffic pattern using standard rejoin procedures.
- Land the aircraft.

Post-Flight Discussion

Most faults are of a random nature and do not form a consistent pattern. Their origin usually lies in rushing the "navigation cycle" as in attempting to locate a small pin point feature without considering anticipated position and large features.

Exercise 19
Flying In Formation

Objective

To teach how to join a formation and hold station, how to change station and how to lead.

Figure 39. Formation flying.

Considerations

General

The high degree of concentration needed when carrying out the exercise is tiring in the early stages. Therefore, the first lessons should be of short duration only and, if necessary, the spacing between aircraft should be more than the customary half wing span.

Before flying solo in formation, the student should be competent at joining formation, breaking formation in an emergency, station keeping, formation changing, and performing an initial approach, break and stream landing. He or she should be capable of adequate leadership, including leading a formation takeoff.

Preparatory Theory

The following matters should be discussed prior to the first formation flight:

- hand signals used in formation;
- basic formation positions;
- position-keeping;
- formation changing;
- taking off and joining formation;
- leading.

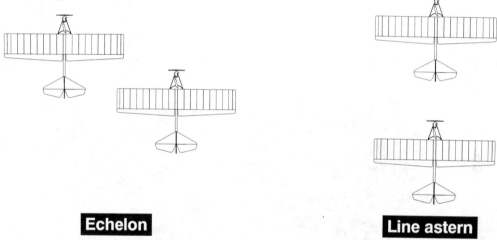

Echelon   Line astern

Figure 40. Basic formations.

Pre-Flight Briefing

This briefing must be comprehensive. The leader's intentions for the whole flight must be outlined and must include the sequence of the changes to be made and also any changes of leader. Each pilot should be allocated a position in the formation, and all responsibilities during formation changes should be detailed.

During Flight

It is advisable for the first practice to consist of only two aircraft, until the student becomes sufficiently competent to manage in larger formations.

Taxiing Out In Formation

The spacing should be such that other aircraft cannot intrude in the procession; but not so close as to be a possible cause of incidents or difficulty in taxiing safely.

Station Keeping

Before starting any instruction in formation flying, it is advisable to allow the student time to settle down and become accustomed to the novelty of the experience.

During the student's first attempts at position-keeping the leader should fly for relatively long periods on a constant heading so as to ease the student's task.

Good formation flying involves the ability to be relaxed while concentrating on position-keeping; it also requires the ability to anticipate the need for control movements and the effect of the movements made. The full use of the natural stability of the aircraft should be stressed.

Figure 41. Line-astern formation.

Breaking and Rejoining Formation

The use of the ailerons to control the distance between aircraft causes a change of heading; the student should be warned of this effect and told to anticipate and make the corrections to the heading in good time.

When joining formation, large throttle and control movements may be required; these should be anticipated to avoid over-controlling.

Changes from the Basic Formation

When moving into line-astern, it is important to anticipate the aileron movement required to position the ultralight correctly; if the aileron movement is not anticipated the aircraft will overshoot the desired position.

Formation Leading

The student should be aware that the leader is responsible for the safety of the formation as a whole in so far as the overall lookout and similar points of airmanship are concerned. The student should also appreciate that the formation leader must be responsible for the navigation of the formation as a whole, but that the fuel state of the "formation flying" aircraft may be less than that of the lead aircraft and must be checked frequently by the pilot.

It should be pointed out that all control movements should be smooth and progressive and that the formation leader's flying should be accurate and considerate at all times. It should be emphasized that all signals should be given in a clear unhurried manner so that they will be easily understood in the formation flying aircraft. Avoid, if possible, forcing the formation flying pilot to look into the sun.

When leading large formations, the leader should remember that the aircraft furthest from the group must make large changes in airspeed, altitude and heading in order to maintain formation; this applies particularly when flying in echelon formation (stepped). Therefore, turns should be entered and completed very gently and the rate of turn kept low.

Airmanship

The student must be constantly aware of the formation and make decisions accordingly. The normal airmanship considerations such as lookout and orientation require more anticipation, while self discipline and knowledge of procedures is of paramount importance. To that end a comprehensive pre-flight briefing is essential.

Air Exercise 19 **Formation Flying**

Technique and Observations

Skill 1: Conduct the formation briefing.

Points which must be included in the formation briefing include:

- Formation call signs, pilots and aircraft.
- Ground and air procedures.
- Exercise.
- Return to field—rejoin traffic pattern and landing.
- Emergencies.

Skill 2: Taxi as a formation.

Leader:
- Taxi with consideration for the formation.
- Check that the formation is ready.
- At the holding point—complete vital actions.

Formation:
- Stay at a correct distance from the aircraft in front.
- Signal when ready.
- At the holding point—line up close to the leader—complete vital actions.

Skill 3: Take off in formation.

Leader:
- Line up, ensure that the formation is ready.
- Signal "brakes off" and open the throttle slowly and smoothly to about three-quarters of full power.
- Make an accurate and smooth takeoff.

Formation:
- Line up in echelon and signal when ready.
- Anticipate leader's throttle opening.
- Keep eye on leader and maintain position.

(continued)

Air Exercise 19 (continued)

Technique and Observations

Skill 4: Lead a formation.

- Responsibility for safety of the formation, look out, fuel, navigation, weather and radio.
- Smooth, accurate flying—with smooth and gradual power changes.
- Signals completed before operation is started.
- Smooth entry and recovery from turns; constant angles of bank.
- Dazzling effect on the sun on the formation.

Skill 5: Fly in formation.

1. Station Keeping—Echelon

- Fly in echelon, spaced one-half wingspan from the leader.
- Appearance and behavior of the other aircraft.
- Correct position vertically, laterally and fore/aft.
- Attention fixed on leader.
- Importance of relaxing.

(a) Elevators:

- Control vertical position.
- Small movements essential.
- Illusion of leader moving.

(b) Aileron and rudder:

- Control lateral spacing—care required.
- Wings parallel to leader's.
- Anticipate removal of bank when closing on leader.
- Small movements essential when in close.
- Use of aileron causes heading changes.
- When in position coordination.

(c) Power:

- Controls fore/aft movement.
- Need to anticipate power changes because of airplane inertia.
- Try to obtain constant throttle setting—avoid over-controlling.

(continued)

Technique and Observations

2. Station Keeping—Line Astern

- Avoid slipstream of aircraft ahead.

  Observations:
- Vertical positioning—angle of sight.
- Horizontal positioning—wings parallel with leader's.
- Fore/aft positioning—one aircraft length behind.

3. Changing Formation

- Drop back clear of leader's tail before crossing.
- Lose altitude to miss propeller slipstream.
- Ensure that there is at least one-half a wingspan or a whole aircraft length between aircraft.
- No violent movements.

4. Turns in Formation

- Maintain the same relative position to the leader.
- Same bank angle as leader.
- Need for change of power on entry and completion of turn.
- Station keeping as for level flight.

5. Breaking and Joining Formation

(a) Breaking:

- Climb so that the leader is hidden under the wing, then break away from the formation and rejoin.
- Positive upward and outward break.
- Danger of rejoining from above.
- Locate the leader—rejoin from behind; stress the importance of rejoining slowly and the anticipation required to allow for aircraft inertia.

(b) Rejoining:

- Initial large throttle movements.
- Use of aileron when well spaced.
- Use of aileron and rudder when close in.
- Systematic adjustment of position—vertical, fore/aft, lateral.

(continued)

Air Exercise 19 (continued)

Technique and Observations

Skill 6: Rejoin a traffic pattern and land as a formation.

- Look out.
- Fly parallel to the runway, just on dead side.
- Echelon away from traffic pattern direction.

Rejoining:
- Initial point about one mile out.
- Be at traffic pattern altitude abeam the runway threshold.

Leader:
- Level breaks made through 90°.
- Downwind turn at normal distance from the runway for an oval pattern.
- Land on left or right-hand side of the runway, depending on the wind direction—usually on the left.

Formation:
- Level break at four-second intervals.
- Downwind leg in long line astern.
- Importance of correct approach speeds.
- Land on alternate sides of runway, or as required.

Post-Flight Discussion

The wing anhedral/dihedral often leads to the student adopting an incorrect level attitude and flying with crossed controls.

Harsh control movements, and over-controlling in general, are usually due to muscular and mental tension; a conscious effort is needed to relax. In the early stages, the instructor should take over control for short periods if it is evident that the student is having trouble in this respect.

Having lost sight of the leader, there is a danger of the student either remaining with the formation or attempting to regain position without first breaking formation and then rejoining.

NOTES

Index